OCD

Free Yourself Triumph Over Negative Emotions Obsessive

(Overcome Obsessive Compulsive Disorder Using Cbt & Dbt Skills for Intrusive Thoughts & Behaviors)

Oscar Barnes

Published By **Frank Joseph**

Oscar Barnes

All Rights Reserved

OCD: Free Yourself Triumph Over Negative Emotions Obsessive (Overcome Obsessive Compulsive Disorder Using Cbt & Dbt Skills for Intrusive Thoughts & Behaviors)

ISBN   978-1-7382957-6-0

Legal & Disclaimer

Table Of Contents

Chapter 1: What Is Ocd?

When humans pay attention the word "OCD," they often photo someone who constantly washes their hands or a person tidy and orderly. These may additionally furthermore without a doubt be a component of OCD in some human beings, but OCD also can show up in quite some approaches which may be regularly a superb deal greater complicated and incapacitating than this.

Recurring mind that get trapped in a person's thoughts and are attempted to be eliminated are called obsessions. These are bothersome, invasive, and continual mind. A character with an obsession is probable to fear approximately the future or experience as although some detail is off. Any situation can also come to be an obsession; some which might be greater normally related to OCD inside the minds of folks that are blind to the ailment encompass counting and germs.

People who have compulsions have interaction in recurrent behaviors to make they experience higher. These might be clean acts, tough workouts and rituals that the character feels compelled to do, or maybe intellectual sports activities. Compulsions embody things like counting, verifying, repeating top notch phrases, and striving for perfection. Youngsters who have compulsions sometimes have interaction their mother and father strongly, relying on them to say or do specific subjects in a totally particular way to feel comfortable. OCD patients think that assignment compulsions are the first-class way to reduce their ache or prevent their fears from materializing.

According to the DSM-5, you need to have compulsions, obsessions, or both to be recognized with OCD. The symptoms and signs and symptoms and symptoms want to be chronic, causing a brilliant deal of pain or useful impairment.

For the victim, OCD is probably very crippling. OCD also can drain someone's time and electricity to the factor of exhaustion (many hours each day). It can also purpose distractions from and/or avoid studying in the school room, finishing assignments on time, being bodily or mentally present with family and buddies, and taking detail in extracurricular sports activities sports.

When a person says some element like "I'm so OCD" once they determine on tidy or easy subjects, many children and teenagers with OCD get indignant with that man or woman. For someone who is struggling with OCD, being attentive to some issue like this may seem very invalidating. Remarks which includes this make the OCD sufferer a lot plenty less possibly to contemplate sharing their opinions with others. Imagine yourself in such pain which you are unable to transport till you contact a door knob collectively together with your left index finger four times. After that, you are pronouncing to yourself twice, "Now the day might be ok."

You repeat this process time and again due to the fact you are uncertain of ways oftentimes to touch the knob and you fear that if you get it incorrect, your mother will go through a terrible destiny that day. Just picture how difficult it is probably to get prepared within the morning for school. That's best a hint of OCD; it's miles going properly beyond clean neatness options. Individuals with out OCD can be beneficial by means of way of being aware about the language they use, due to the fact you in no manner recognize whether the man or woman sitting next to you is experiencing OCD symptoms and signs and symptoms.

OCD is treatable, and help is to be had. Exposure and Response Prevention (ERP) is a form of Cognitive Behavioral Therapy that is most customarily used to address OCD. With ERP, someone can also learn how to confront their OCD often without giving in to its compulsions and obsessions. While doing this on your non-public may be very difficult, looking for the assist of an authorized mental fitness professional may make it less complicated.

ERP gives you the potential to regain control over your mind, emotions, and behaviors. OCD is similar to a highbrow trick that makes humans do not forget horrible matters will arise if remarkable matters are not notion or finished. Effective ERP requires self-control, hobby, and exercising each outside and inside of remedy instructions. In addition to presenting assist, buddies and circle of relatives can also moreover resource by means of using abstaining from OCD rituals.

Even with ERP therapy, development ought to once in a while lag. Some sufferers find out that in addition to seeing a psychiatrist, taking remedy helps them deal with their OCD. Verify the psychiatrist's history in treating OCD sufferers earlier than choosing one.

The Real Deal With Teenage OCD.

The abbreviation OCD, which stands for obsessive-compulsive ailment, is now often used in communique. When someone describes their choice for subjects to be in a awesome way, they'll label themselves as OCD patients. On the alternative hand, obsessive-compulsive disorder is a real intellectual contamination that manifests as extreme issues and compulsive hobby. For this purpose, dad and mom and teens should be privy to the realities surrounding OCD.

Anxiety problems together with OCD have an effect on someone's capability to feature in everyday existence, at work, in relationships, and education.

The unwelcome and unsettling thoughts, photographs, or cravings that symbolize an obsessive-compulsive infection sufferer are known as obsessions. Extreme anxiety is due to those obsessions.

Compulsions, from time to time called OCD rituals, are repeated mind or sports activities that an OCD sufferer does to reduce anxiety. They frequently sense pressured to carry out these moves all day prolonged.

Consequently, the signs and symptoms of obsessive-compulsive disorder become time-eating and cause intellectual discomfort. The person isn't always capable of forestall oneself, despite the truth that they may be aware that their movements and concerns are unreasonable.

OCD regularly progresses over the years if remedy isn't obtained. Therefore, if OCD signs and signs and signs and symptoms appear, they need to be evaluated right away by way of the usage of a qualified intellectual fitness expert.

Fact #1: Anxiety troubles embody OCD.

OCD is classed as an anxiety infection, and symptoms of generalized anxiety disorder are frequently discovered in OCD sufferers. OCD sufferers can also moreover have extreme anxieties and compulsive demanding thoughts. Suicidal thoughts and moves are some specific hazard issue associated with OCD.

Fact #2: The important signs of OCD are compulsions and obsessions.

An OCD sufferer gets passionate about high-quality phobias or aversions that they experience often. Some issues, like being ill or doing poorly on an examination, also can make revel in. However, compared to normal, the obsessive thoughts' frequency and depth are lots greater excessive.

OCD patients' unreasonable response to their obsessions and anxieties is the improvement of compulsions. An obsessive-compulsive disease (OCD) sufferer believes that by means of manner of manner of repeating a habitual or action—like counting or hand washing—the scary stop end result will now not materialize.

OCD compulsions and obsessions regularly in shape into this type of four schooling of OCD behaviors:

Examining Mental Contamination and Contamination

Amassing ruminating or bothersome thoughts

List of Symptoms of OCD

Teens affected by obsessive-compulsive disorder can also revel in excruciating ache, ache, and terror. Moreover, their behavior is complex to others, who do now not understand why they may be unable to control their compulsions.

Here are some precise instances of OCD obsessions and workout exercises.

Obsessions with OCD

Fearing for one's fitness or safety

Dislike of dirt or pathogens

Taboo thoughts on violence and sex

Aggressive mind directed towards oneself or different people

Concerned about the safety of your self or a cherished one

Worry approximately pollution within the environment, such asbestos

obsession with not unusual home chemical substances like solvents and cleansers

Fear of blurting forth curses and obscenities

Fearful of with the aid of accident hurting someone

Unable to detail with gadgets which can be preceding or nugatory

the need that devices be located in a fantastic way

OCD Habits

Checking once more certain the oven is off or a door is secured, as an instance

Frequently studying one's body or individual components,

Reading and rewriting over again

repeating every day movements, together with beginning and remaining doorways

Hand washing too much

Putting objects in a selected series and association, which include consuming meals in a certain order

Routinely tidying oneself or one's possessions

An obsession with counting

Carrying out moves in multiple, together with putting in and remaining doorways three instances.

Having To Follow Strict Guidelines

OCD Seizures

Another sign of OCD is a tic hassle. Tics are in particular described as abrupt, fleeting, repeated motions. These could probably consist of the following:

blinking of the eyes and distinct eye motions

smirking

a shrug of the shoulders

jerking the shoulders or head

Vocal tics encompass persistent clearing of the throat, sniffing, or grunting.

Fact #three: Late formative years is whilst OCD is regularly identified.

The late adolescent years are at the same time as OCD diagnoses are most not unusual. OCD is regularly diagnosed earlier than the age of nineteen, with 25% of instances recognized earlier than the age of 14. Towards early maturity, there may be a decline in the chance of OCD.

Furthermore, in some unspecified time in the future of puberty, there is an equal chance for boys and girls to gather OCD. On the alternative hand, OCD is extra not unusual among boys subsequently of adolescence.

What is the prevalence of OCD?

According to the National Institute of Mental Health (NIMH), about 1 in 50 Americans, or 2.Three% of the populace, be through obsessive-compulsive ailment (OCD).

Fact #4: Overanalyzing and perfectionism are not the most effective additives of OCD.

Obsessive thinking manifests itself in lots of forms, alongside side the urge to double-test items or set up their surroundings in a specific way. On the alternative hand, OCD is not just like being smooth and tidy or being a perfectionist.

Adolescents tormented by OCD commonly have compulsive mind and behaviors for at least an hour consistent with day. Furthermore, even after knowing that their recurrent mind and moves are excessive, they may be now not able to prevent them. In addition, people can also enjoy fleeting moments of respite after rituals, however the ones obsessive moves deliver them no pleasure. A in addition indication of adolescent OCD is while the signs and symptoms and signs and symptoms adversely have an effect at the adolescent's daily sports activities.

How Can You Tell Whether It's OCD?

What if you suspect OCD for your adolescent? To diagnose adolescent OCD, a mental medical medical doctor need to behavior an OCD screening. A highbrow exam is a part of an OCD assessment to talk approximately the volume of the character's compulsive behaviors and obsessive mind. A mental health expert or scientific physician may additionally use standards covered within the Diagnostic and Statistical Manual of Mental Disorders (DSM-five). Additionally, they must rule out any medical situations or physical problems that would be developing or exacerbating OCD-like behaviors and mind.

Fact #five: Anxiety problems regularly run in families.

Despite the shortage of 1, obvious etiology for OCD, scientists had been looking for to determine if the contamination is inherited. It has been validated that those who have an OCD- determine, sibling, or teenager are much more likely to have OCD themselves. Additionally, there may be a more hazard that the relative had OCD as a teen or teen. The relationship among genetics and OCD continues to be being investigated in ongoing research inclusive of twins and households.

OCD hazard elements can also additionally encompass versions inside the shape and feature of the mind. In particular, researchers have decided versions inside the brain's frontal cortex and subcortical areas in OCD patients. They hence assume there can be a link amongst anomalies in advantageous thoughts areas and OCD signs and symptoms and symptoms. The International OCD Foundation is one organisation that helps ongoing research into the reasons of OCD.

Fact #6: Experiencing trauma as a little one may moreover boom your threat of having OCD.

Studies mean that those with a records of youth trauma, in particular emotional forget about or physical, emotional, or sexual abuse, are much more likely to expand obsessive-compulsive disease (OCD). Moreover, a 2021 studies located that human beings with OCD who had worrying reviews as kids had been more likely to broaden sadness further to extra severe OCD signs and signs and symptoms and signs and symptoms.

Furthermore, OCD or related symptoms and symptoms may additionally additionally additionally emerge in children with Pediatric Autoimmune Neuropsychiatric Disorders Associated with Streptococcal Infections (PANDAS), a form of streptococcal contamination.

Fact #7: OCD and wonderful intellectual health problems are cautiously associated.

Teens who be bothered by way of manner of OCD signs and symptoms frequently moreover be via different intellectual ailments, like:

Chapter 2: Inhibitors Of Serotonin Reuptake

SSRIs, or selective serotonin reuptake inhibitors, Clomipramine, an antidepressant from the sooner "tricyclic" elegance,

Antipsychotic capsules

Treatment Options for OCD Research has examined that Cognitive Behavioral Therapy (CBT) is powerful in decreasing signs and symptoms and signs and symptoms and signs of OCD.

Exposure and Response Prevention (ERP), a sort of cognitive behavioral remedy, is useful in lowering obsessive inclinations.

Acceptance similarly to self-control

The signs and signs of OCD may be dealt with with treatment.

Deep brain stimulation (DBS) includes implanting electrodes within the brain to supply impulses that help manage of mind feature. This remedy is in particular implemented for sufferers over the age of 18.

Transcranial magnetic stimulation is a few distinctive approach for reducing the symptoms and signs of OCD (TMS). TMS stimulates thoughts nerve cells by using the use of way of the use of magnetic fields.

Everything about OCD

OCD stands for obsessive-compulsive ailment. The continual, crippling medical contamination referred to as obsessive-compulsive disorder (OCD) is characterised via compulsions and obsessions. Compulsions are compulsive sports that someone feels compelled to perform to reduce the suffering that their obsessions cause. Obsessions are unwelcome, scary thoughts, photographs, or urges that continuously circulate someone's thoughts.

Compulsions, but, aren't continuously enjoyable, frequently take a first rate deal of time, and seldom purpose the accomplishment of a worthwhile goal.

OCD ought to not be unsuitable with obsessive-compulsive person ailment (OCPD), irrespective of the opportunity of sure signs and symptoms being similar in a few activities.

Despite its name, obsessions and compulsions aren't a part of OCPD. A man or woman disorder is called OCPD is characterized via a chronic sample of conduct that consists of an obsession with order and consists of developments like perfectionism and tension.

Crucially, each of those troubles have the capacity to noticeably harm the affected person as well as others with whom they have got connections. OCD patients aren't frequently OCPD.

WHAT IS THE CAUSE OF OCD?

OCD does no longer have a single, set up etiology. Multifactorial causation indicates that each hereditary and environmental variables are possibly at play.

The extended-held belief that OCD resulted best from existence activities has been antique with the resource of manner of the mounting proof that neurological variables play a major characteristic inside the infection. Research shows that negative communication a number of the orbital cortex, located inside the the the the front of the mind, and the basal ganglia, located within the deeper thoughts areas, can be related to OCD. Serotonin is a neurotransmitter—a chemical "messenger" amongst nerve cells—that is used by sure thoughts areas. It is concept that a awesome contributing trouble to OCD is a low serotonin degree. In OCD, dopamine systems may be worried.

An possibility speculation posits that OCD is related to numerous car-immune responses, wherein the frame's safety machine in opposition to infection goals healthful tissue.

The truth that OCD may additionally additionally moreover every now and then begin in infancy and be linked to strep throat—a painful throat brought on via manner of a streptococcus bacterial infection—gives evidence in want of this concept.

According to analyze, the quantity of genes may additionally moreover impact the ailment's development and heredity can also on occasion play a detail in its onset. Even even though genetic connections are nevertheless being researched globally—as an example, the worldwide Obsessive Compulsive Foundation Genetics Consortium these days collaborated to perform an entire genome association test on DNA samples from OCD patients from anywhere inside the worldwide—there is strong evidence that OCD does now and again run in households, with equal twins having a 70% danger of having the disease.

WHO IS AT RISK AND WHO GETS OCD?

The occurrence of OCD is quite high, affecting 1% to 3.Three% of the population.

From preschool age to maturity, onset also can seem at any second (usually before the age of 40 years).

In evaluation to ladies, who frequently have signs in their overdue teenagers or early twenties, men commonly begin experiencing symptoms as youngsters or teenagers. Between one-1/three and fifty in keeping with cent of person OCD patients say that their condition originated in youngsters. It influences every women and men almost similarly regularly.

There is a small boom inside the risk that a baby may additionally have OCD if one of the dad and mom does.

But such customs are not passed down thru families. For example, a woman who washes obsessively and has contamination anxieties may additionally additionally produce a child who has ritualistic checking.

OCD is a condition that influences humans of all persona types and isn't always specially associated with stress or intellectual conflict. It's interesting to word that quite some patients declare that as their pressure degrees upward push, their OCD (severity, pain, disability) rises as well (e.G. Before or within the path of assessments).

Hormonal functioning also can doubtlessly have an effect on OCD. Hormones might also moreover have a widespread characteristic in the development or expression of OCD, specifically in girls. For example, a number of ladies record having more obsessive-compulsive (OC) symptoms and signs and symptoms during their premenstrual or menstrual durations, or that their OCD symptoms commenced in the path of being pregnant or soon after giving begin. For fantastic women, the start of OCD may additionally additionally coincide with menopause.

Mood troubles which incorporates bipolar affective sickness (manic depression) and sadness regularly coexist with OCD. Research on scientific samples has established that between 29.6% and 43% of OCD patients also be concerned by comorbid depression.

This will growth the diploma of impairment associated with OCD. Studies have additionally proven a link some of the co-prevalence of OCD and depression and the diagnosis, terrible reaction to remedy, and chronicity and severity of OCD signs and symptoms and signs and symptoms.

OCD Symptoms and Signs

Obsessions and compulsions are regularly observed in OCD patients, but now and again simplest one of them can also rise up.

Recurrent and chronic thoughts, urges, or visions that a person feels not capable of prevent or regulate are referred to as obsessions. Most humans see obsessions as absurd, unsettling, and bothersome, and they are trying to cowl or brush aside them. The obsessions are frequently discovered by using manner of doubts, worry, anxiety, or revulsion.

Excessive problem approximately dirt or germs and the possibility which you might probable become inflamed or contaminate others

Feeling that you have harm yourself or incredible people; wondering protection precautions (which include making sure the burner is off);

Thinking that a horrible event will show up or that you can perform a bit aspect horrible

Intruding thoughts of sexuality;

Obsessive symmetry or the urge to have the entirety "sincerely so";

Intruding violent or disgusting imagery

Overwhelming moral or religious disgrace or uncertainty; obvious visions of blasphemy

An immoderate amount of hesitancy or doubt: "Should I or want to not I?"

The want to show, inquire, or admit

Obsessions:

Conversely, compulsive behaviors are characterized as ritualistic, repeating moves of concept or conduct which might be regularly finished with the beneficial aid of predetermined "guidelines"

Cleaning or washing: such as giving yourself many showers or scrubbing your palms till they emerge as painfully crimson.

Chapter 3: How Can Ocd Are Identified?

OCD is regularly underdiagnosed. People with intellectual ailments may additionally cover their signs and symptoms and symptoms and signs and dispose of getting remedy from a professional due to this stigma. The description of OCD as a "secretive infection" is not unexpected.

It's moreover possible for OCD sufferers to be ignorant that they've a diagnosable, curable circumstance. This situation is enhancing as a surrender cease end result of recent media campaigns, intellectual fitness agencies, and stigmatization responsibilities. However, some clinical practitioners are though unaware of the signs and symptoms of OCD.

OCD cannot be identified with laboratory trying out; as an opportunity, analysis is made thru comparing your signs and signs and symptoms. In addition to questioning you and frequently others near you approximately your signs and symptoms and symptoms and symptoms, your clinical medical doctor will mainly inquire about the forms of obsessions or compulsions you go through. Additionally, you'll be requested how an awful lot time you spend every day sporting out workouts or obsessing. (For example, you could have OCD if you spend more than an hour a day conducting pointless carrying activities.)

Additionally, your scientific doctor will ensure that no prescription or drug you may be taking within the period in-between is nerve-racking your signs and symptoms and signs and signs and symptoms and signs and symptoms.

MANAGEMENT METHODS FOR OCD

The maximum a fulfillment treatment for OCD is a aggregate of antidepressant remedy and cognitive-behavioral therapy (CBT). OCD treatment calls for a sustained dedication. Although it may take many months for both shape of remedy to begin operating, great outcomes are often seen rapid. Recuperation is predicated upon seriously on the affected man or woman's self-control to and active involvement in remedy, similarly to on the assist of his or her family and a sturdy, sincere healing alliance.

Drugs

The most usually given capsules for OCD are selective serotonin reuptake inhibitors (SSRIs), which might be antidepressants. Examples of these pills consist of citalopram (Cipramil), paroxetine (Aropax), fluoxetine (Prozac), sertraline (Zoloft), and fluvoxamine (Luvox).

Another medication that is carried out is clomipramine, additionally known as Anafranil. This selective serotonin inhibitor influences special neurotransmitters similarly to serotonin and might have extra lousy outcomes.

Most individuals discover it much less hard to cope with SSRIs. While every of these antidepressants works truly as well, there may be a certain individual for whom one drug works higher than some different.

The majority of patients get some comfort from the ones drugs after four to 6 weeks, however it's miles important to provide the treatment a whole 10 to twelve weeks to decide whether or no longer or now not it's far powerful. Your medical doctor can also attempt decreasing the dosage, adding greater remedy, or switching to some other treatment in case you do have horrifying side effects.

It is viable to strive a brand new SSRI if the modern-day

one has showed unsuccessful after 10 to 12 weeks of remedy.

As an opportunity, the primary medicine may be blended with any other, or adding CBT would possibly beautify the efficacy of the course of remedy.

Crucially important: Your therapist need to verify that the remedy has been administered in a sufficient quantity of time and at a massive enough dosage earlier than concluding that it has failed.

Since plenty much less than 20% of sufferers dealt with with remedy on my own can also additionally additionally have entire symptom decision, remedy and cognitive behavioral treatment are regularly used in conjunction for superior consequences. Depending in your age and the severity of your OCD, you may want to take medicinal drug.

If cognitive behavioral treatment (CBT) is not a success in treating milder instances of OCD, treatment may be administered. Medication is regularly the primary line of treatment for people with intense OCD or co-taking place issues (which encompass melancholy), and CBT is added at the same time as the drugs starts to paintings.

Physicians are much more likely to lease CBT by myself while treating greater younger patients. Medication that could be implemented in desire to an authorized cognitive behavioral psychotherapist is not reachable.

Cognitive-behavioral remedy (CBT): Behavior remedy teaches you to modify your thoughts to regulate your emotions and conduct.

Cognitive treatment and publicity and response prevention (E/RP) are additives of behavior remedy for OCD.

These upgrades need to be sustained till OCD signs and signs and symptoms and signs are simply long past or substantially diminished. When looking to give up remedy or cognitive behavioral therapy, the majority of professionals recommend at least six months of month-to-month observe-up schooling and no longer lots much less than a yr of ongoing remedy.

Withdrawing from medicine may additionally result in relapse, in particular if CBT has now not been acquired. If you are unable to get CBT, it's miles suggested which you maintain taking your medicinal drug.

Individuals with recurrent OCD episodes should need extended-term prophylactic (preventative) therapy.

The majority of medical doctors advise grade by grade preventing remedy at the same time as attending CBT booster lessons to avoid relapse in case you do not require prolonged-time period remedy. It is more hard to alter OCD after it's far beneath control, so do no longer lessen or prevent your treatment without first seeing your scientific health practitioner.

Knowledge and the help of family

Engage your family for your remedy, and inform all of us who can be affected approximately the illness. This will guarantee which you get the first-class care and help you in handling your OCD.

Joining a help institution might probably help you find out new coping mechanisms for OCD and make you revel in plenty less by myself.

Family people may assist an man or woman with OCD who refuses to get treatment or rejects the assessment via making sure they've get admission to to facts regarding the situation and permitting them to recognise that there are effective treatment alternatives available.

Other family humans can also get engrossed in the physical games of the amusing seeker, which also can bring about massive disruptions from OCD. Family contributors may additionally look at from the therapist a manner to regularly distance themselves from them.

Chapter 4: Understanding Ocd

On event, it is everyday to move once more and double-check that the Electric Cooker is unplugged, to be concerned which you were infected with the beneficial aid of germs, or to have an unsightly, violent idea. However, when you have obsessive-compulsive sickness (OCD), obsessive thoughts and compulsive behaviors can turn out to be so overwhelming that they intrude alongside side your each day lifestyles.

OCD is described thru uncontrollable, undesirable thoughts and ritualized, repetitive behaviors that you are feeling pressured to engage in. If you have got got OCD, you're likely conscious that your obsessive mind and compulsive behaviors are irrational, however you're but now not capable of face up to them and damage free.

Like a needle caught on an antique record, OCD reasons the thoughts to come to be fixated on a particular concept or urge. For example, you could take a look at the range

30 times to ensure that it's far actually grew to grow to be off due to the fact you are scared of burning down your property, or you can scrub your fingers uncooked out of fear of germs. While performing the ones repetitive behaviors does now not convey you pleasure, they'll offer a few temporary treatments from the anxiety due to obsessive mind.

You may additionally furthermore try and avoid conditions that reason or exacerbate your signs and symptoms and signs, or you can use alcohol or drugs to self-medicate. While it can appear which you can't escape your obsessions and compulsions, there are numerous matters you can do to interrupt free from undesirable mind and irrational urges and regain manage of your thoughts and moves.

Historically, OCD modified into labeled as an anxiety disorder below the Diagnostic and Statistical Manual of Mental Disorders (DSM). Nevertheless, OCD modified into moved out of the "Anxiety Disorders" section of the DSM within the fifth version, and a modern section named "Obsessive-Compulsive and Related Conditions" modified into brought.

The exchange modified into made after researchers discovered vast versions among OCD and anxiety issues. For instance, with OCD, you respond to unwanted mind with repetitive, vain rituals. You may additionally moreover or might not be aware that your mind and compulsions, together with not unusual hand washing, are irrational. However, tension reasons you to ruminate on actual-worldwide troubles, which includes a fear of being mocked or judged. You can also moreover reply with the aid of preserving off the supply of your worry, but you can no longer use fantastic rituals to alleviate your misery.

Certain remedies for OCD and anxiety problems may furthermore variety. To cope with an anxiety ailment, you may need to grade by grade confront your fears, while treating OCD requires addressing the compulsive behavior.

Obsessions are involuntary mind, photos, or impulses that repeat on your mind. You don't want to have those mind, but you cannot avoid them. Unfortunately, those obsessive mind are regularly disruptive and distracting.

Compulsions are behaviors or rituals that you are feeling compelled to copy over and over. Compulsions are typically used to alleviate obsessions. For example, in case you're worried about infection, you can increase complicated cleansing rituals. However, the comfort does no longer remaining. In truth, obsessive mind regularly return more potent. Compulsive rituals and behaviors regularly purpose anxiety as they end up greater annoying and time-ingesting, that is a vicious cycle of OCD.

Hoarding & OCD

Hoarding changed into formerly categorized as an OCD disorder. While estimates propose that up to 25% of human beings with OCD interact in compulsive hoarding, it may furthermore be a symptom of a separate situation, hoarding infection.

Hoarders are afraid that throwing some thing away will bring about a few element horrible, so that they keep things they do now not need or use. However, there can be a difference amongst OCD-associated hoarding and hoarding disease.

OCD-related hoarders do not collect so many possessions that their homes emerge as unmanageable. Hoarding is commonly unwelcome and distressing for them, serving as a technique of managing intrusive mind.

In assessment, a person with hoarding sickness reviews each excessive first-class and terrible emotions. Acquiring possessions brings satisfaction in desire to absolutely alluring a compulsion, and being surrounded thru their property gives comfort. The distress in hoarding disorder is introduced approximately greater by using the results of hoarding—muddle and an unsafe environment—in addition to the tension of having to discard possessions.

The Four Categories of OCD

Obsessions and compulsions can contain a extensive type of topics. However, the bulk of them fall into 4 training. You can also additionally have obsessive thoughts and compulsions that suit into multiple instructions. You also can have obsessions and compulsions that range from those indexed under.

Unacceptable or taboo mind

Persons with this shape of OCD have intrusive thoughts that are irrelevant for his or her values, whether or not or no longer or not sexual, violent, or taboo. Everyone may moreover have an "unacceptable" notion every now and then. However, human beings with OCD can also have a more difficult time letting those thoughts drift. "Taboo" mind regularly revolve spherical a few fundamental problems, on the side of:

Sexual orientation OCD

These intrusive mind/obsessions center on the individual's sexual orientation. They can also regularly question their sexual enchantment to others. And they will are attempting to find for reassurance from others about their sexual orientation on a everyday foundation.

Relationship OCD

It isn't uncommon to have moments of doubt in a relationship. But relationship OCD extends beyond the ones commonplace concerns. It may additionally moreover moreover reason a person to continuously query whether or not or now not or no longer they're in a courting with the "right" individual. They may additionally end up fixated on their partner's "flaws" and character traits.

OCD motives harm

Someone with OCD is worried about their capability or willingness to harm others. They can also injure themselves, their loved ones, or maybe a stranger due to this fear. It will be discovered by way of annoying violent snap shots or thoughts.

Pedophilia OCD

These intrusive mind/obsessions stem from fears of being sexually inquisitive about or harming youngsters. Even if there is no evidence to back up this suspicion, the character might also moreover additionally have distressing doubts about being a pedophile.

Scrupulosity OCD

A man or woman with OCD that suits this issue remember range may additionally additionally constantly reveal themselves for "immoral" or "sinful" behavior, mind, or feelings. Their intrusive mind and obsessions are approximately moral, moral, or spiritual problems.

People with taboo obsessions may additionally additionally display off much less obvious compulsions. They frequently interact in distinct styles of compulsions to relieve their anxiety, together with:

Thought suppression or deliberately trying not to have a idea.

Seeking guarantee from others.

Obsessively praying

These thoughts are particularly frightening due to the fact they do not reflect the character's values. In elegant, someone with OCD will keep away from committing the acts they fear. Instead, they'll go to tremendous lengths to avoid having those mind.

Doubt and Double-Checking

People with OCD regularly lack believe of their private reminiscence and judgment. Doubt is a key element of all forms of OCD. However, a few human beings have a specially difficult time doubting their very

very own belief of truth. They also can moreover doubt their potential to recollect cutting-edge sports activities.

A person with this form of OCD can also furthermore go away the residence, lock their door, and then wonder if they in truth locked their door once they get into their automobile. This may be a common enjoy for plenty people. However, a person with OCD may additionally moreover additionally need to check once more numerous times in advance than trusting that the assignment is whole.

Another feature of OCD is incompleteness or the feeling that some element isn't always "simply right". For example, someone with OCD can also lock their door time and again. Even if the door became properly locked the first time, this sense of incompleteness can pressure them to copy the venture until it feels "actually proper."

Chapter 5: The Effects Of Ocd On Daily Life

People with Obsessive-Compulsive Disorder are in a consistent country of distress due to intrusive mind and accompanying compulsions aimed in the direction of reducing tension, which in the long run impacts their excellent of existence. Obsessions and compulsions may additionally have a good sized effect on one's outstanding of life, making even number one responsibilities tough. Here are some of the techniques that OCD ought to have an effect on unique additives of your lifestyles:

Personal and Social Relationships

One of the most tough components of dwelling with OCD is its impact on private and social relationships. Individuals with OCD may additionally war to engage in social sports activities or hold relationships due to the time-ingesting nature of compulsions. Fear of being judged or misunderstood thru way of others also can result in isolation and loneliness.

Furthermore, OCD can placed a strain on own family relationships. It may be tough for family contributors to understand the man or woman's compulsive conduct and disability to manipulate their obsessions. This lack of knowledge can motive tension, conflict, and emotional misery in the family.

Performance

OCD has a huge impact on academic and occupational widespread overall overall performance. Students with OCD also can conflict to popularity on their research because of normal obsessions. They may additionally spend a huge amount of time appearing rituals, which impedes their academic improvement.

Similarly, humans with OCD can also have problem being effective at paintings. They can also conflict to meet closing dates or entire responsibilities efficaciously because of the time spent on compulsions. Obsession-related anxiety also can make it tough to recognition, resulting in bad typical performance.

Overwhelming doubts

Individuals with Obsessive-Compulsive Disorder have trouble concentrating because of excessive doubt. Compulsions are regularly used to relieve the ones doubts; for instance, a cleanliness obsession might also cause excessive handwashing.

Interference with Daily Life

Perfectionism is a commonplace trait in OCD sufferers, making even smooth duties difficult because of a loss of cognizance and unrealistic expectations. Obsessive-Compulsive Disorder disrupts ordinary lifestyles thru causing anxiety and interfering with ordinary responsibilities.

Disturbance in relationships

OCD can stress relationships because of the reality people name for unique behaviors from cherished ones and are continuously worried approximately their nicely-being. Family participants who apprehend the man or woman of OCD are better able to offer help. Education about the disorder allows to dispel myths and foster empathy.

Self-Harm

Ritualistic compulsions to alleviate anxiety can result in self-damage, which incorporates deciding on at hair or pores and skin in some unspecified time in the future of intrusive mind. Excessive hand washing also can cause pores and skin problems.

Consuming Drugs

Some human beings may additionally use pills or engage in particular sports activities to cope with persistent horrible thoughts and the preference to carry out actions to relieve anxiety resulting from repetitive perception patterns.

Physical Health

OCD is usually a intellectual health sickness, however it may also have a bodily impact. Chronic pressure and tension from OCD can reason severa physical health problems, collectively with complications, gastrointestinal problems, and fatigue. Furthermore, compulsive behaviors like immoderate washing can cause bodily harm, along side pores and pores and pores and skin inflammation or harm.

Emotional Wellbeing

Finally, and perhaps most importantly, OCD has a tremendous impact on emotional well-being. Constantly wrestling with intrusive mind may be exceptionally distressing, resulting in emotions of frustration, guilt, and melancholy. OCD's persistent nature, mixed with the issue of managing signs and symptoms, can result in the improvement of other mental health issues which encompass depression or anxiety problems.

Common myths about OCD coping abilities

There are some commonplace myths about OCD coping talents that can be deceptive and prevent people from effectively managing their condition. Here, we address some of these misconceptions by using the usage of providing clean and accurate statistics.

OCD coping talents can remedy OCD genuinely

While OCD coping abilities are crucial for handling signs and symptoms and signs and symptoms and enhancing excellent of lifestyles, they're no longer a remedy for OCD. The aim is to assist humans live with their state of affairs extra without problems and with out being too disrupted with the aid of their signs and symptoms and signs and signs.

OCD coping talents are same to normal stress management techniques

While a few OCD coping techniques can also moreover overlap with famous stress manage strategies, they will be first-rate. OCD coping talents are designed to deal with the unique annoying situations of OCD, which include intrusive thoughts and compulsive actions.

OCD coping talents are best effective in therapy

While treatment can provide a installed and guided surroundings for studying and education OCD coping competencies, those talents additionally can be used independently. They are designed to be realistic equipment that people with OCD can use to manipulate their symptoms at any time and from any location.

OCD coping competencies are sincerely about suppressing obsessive thoughts

Contrary to famous perception, many OCD coping strategies contain acknowledging and accepting mind, in vicinity of suppressing them. Mindfulness and cognitive reframing strategies, as an example, reason to exchange the connection with obsessive mind in area of get rid of them.

Seeking Professional Diagnosis and Assessment.

It is crucial to recognize that there may be no unmarried kind of OCD assessment. Different types of assessments can be more or lots a great deal much less suitable primarily based at the person's wishes and occasions. There are specifically four varieties of OCD tests, which encompass:

Clinical Interview

A installation medical interview is a commonplace method of assessing OCD. This is usually finished with a intellectual health expert, which includes a psychiatrist, psychologist, or medical social employee. It includes asking inquiries concerning your symptoms and signs, mind, and moves.

Furthermore, this kind allows to rule out each other intellectual fitness troubles that might be causing your signs and symptoms and symptoms. The interviewer will ask questions about the character with OCD. They may even inquire about one-of-a-kind components of functioning, collectively with employment and relationships. Eventually, inside the path of those interviews, a intellectual health expert will problem a analysis.

Self-record measures

Self-record measures are each different way to assess OCD. This can take the form of a paper and pencil questionnaire or a web survey. It typically asks about your signs and symptoms and symptoms and the way they have got affected your existence. Self-document measures are usually used to show for OCD and show symptoms and symptoms and symptoms over the years. They moreover can be used to determine the severity of OCD signs, which is known as a mental evaluation.

Observational measures

Observational measures are another manner to assess OCD. This commonly consists of looking at the person with OCD in numerous situations, which include in some unspecified time in the future of a conversation or at the same time as performing a project. More often, this includes searching on the person perform hard sports activities or obligations, collectively with cleaning or organizing. The clinician can then look for any patterns or issues that can exist.

The observer will hold song of any unusual behaviors or mannerisms. They can also inquire approximately the character's thoughts and emotions regarding their obsessive-compulsive behaviors. Observational measures can help take a look at the severity of OCD signs and symptoms and the manner they've an impact on the man or woman's life.

Chapter 6: Root Causes Of Ocd

Although OCD affects a large form of people, its underlying reasons are not truely understood. On the other hand, a aggregate of environment, mind chemistry, and heredity is idea to be responsible. Here are some elements that have been related to OCD and may worsen or boom the chance of signs and signs and symptoms in people who are susceptible to the illness:

Upbringing

Helicopter dad and mom are much more likely to be overprotective, which may additionally additionally increase some kid's vulnerability to OCD. Other capacity chance elements for growing OCD embody having numerous duty as a baby or being subjected to extremely strict pointers. Stressful or distressing situations can purpose or worsen signs and symptoms and symptoms in parents which can be predisposed to OCD.

It stays too early to attract definitive conclusions about the ones links and the way genes may additionally moreover moreover engage with early life reviews to growth the risk of developing OCD. We recognise masses approximately addressing OCD once it's miles identified, but little about how or even as it develops.

Sleep conduct and patterns

Yes, loss of sleep exacerbates all signs and symptoms, together with OCD. Your bedtime and sleep period count on your potential to govern or withstand obsessive thoughts. In a 2018 have a take a look at posted in Sleep, humans with OCD who went to mattress after middle of the night had a extra tough time controlling obsessive mind. Furthermore, a 2018 check published in the Journal of Behavior Therapy and Experimental Psychiatry determined that those who sleep less than the encouraged 8 hours in step with night are much more likely to experience intrusive, repetitive thoughts. Light container remedy might also moreover additionally help to reset circadian rhythms and improve the terrific and amount of sleep. The studies is ongoing, but sitting within the the the front of a slight place for half-hour consistent with day can assist circulate the sleep cycle in advance and reduce OCD symptoms and signs and signs and signs. Lightboxes are commonly safe, however they have to no longer be used by people who've precise eye troubles or are touchy to daylight hours.

Brain inflammation

Scientists may moreover furthermore have located one functionality factor contributing to OCD contamination. According to a 2017 have a look at posted in JAMA Psychiatry, mind scans of people with OCD observed out that contamination have become 32% higher in six mind areas recognized to play a function in OCD than in the ones without OCD. Furthermore, preceding research in the Journal of Neuroinflammation indicates that brain inflammation also can furthermore play a characteristic in unique psychiatric conditions which consist of predominant depressive disease, schizophrenia, and bipolar ailment. If researchers can discover a manner to lessen the terrible aspect outcomes of inflammation, it is able to help within the development of remedies for the ones situations.

Fear of Losing Control

People with OCD may additionally experience forced to double-check things like turning off the range and locking the door. According to investigate, a fear of dropping manage can be linked to the checking behaviors that constitute OCD. In a 2017 have a have a examine posted in the Journal of Obsessive-Compulsive and Related Disorders, psychology researchers checked out a hundred thirty+ university college university students and suggested some, but now not others, that they had been at greater risk of losing control over their thoughts and movements based mostly on "EEG proof." In a lab check in which individuals had to regulate the rate of photos, people who believed they were at better risk of losing manipulate had been instances as probable to double-check which keys to apply as folks that did no longer consider they have been liable to dropping manage. The researchers hypothesized that people's fear and beliefs about losing manipulate could placed them at hazard for a number of psychiatric problems, which includes OCD, generalized anxiety sickness, and panic infection, among others.

Your exposure to particular forms of bacteria

Pediatric autoimmune neuropsychiatric issues related to streptococcal infections (PANDAS) are seeking advice from the uncommon, sudden, and dramatic onset of OCD and/or tic problems following a strep contamination, or the worsening of such after a strep infection. According to the International OCD Foundation, PANDAS maximum usually influences youngsters aged four to fourteen years. It takes area even as the immune machine misfires in response to a strep contamination and attacks the mind.

According to the National Institute of Mental Health, treating strep with antibiotics is the exceptional way to fight PANDAS. While they will step by step fade after remedy, signs and signs and symptoms can also reappear if strep returns. Because PANDAS is so unusual, many specific opportunities must be taken into consideration earlier than a evaluation is made.

Your strain or pent-up anger

No, anger does now not purpose OCD. However, whilst someone with OCD internalizes anger and rage, their signs and symptoms and signs and symptoms may also worsen. ''Internalized anger, if not expressed, which incorporates through communique, exercise, or every different outlet, have to circulate somewhere, regularly main to despair, anxiety, and OCD. OCD flares aren't uncommon throughout annoying or irritated times. Seeking treatment is crucial as researchers try to apprehend the reason of OCD. OCD can be appreciably debilitating, however there are remedies available. Cognitive conduct remedy, communicate remedy, and capsules can all be powerful in treating OCD.

Your worry of guilt

According to a 2017 have a observe posted inside the magazine Clinical Psychology & Psychotherapy, OCD can be encouraged via an severe fear of guilt. The researchers decided that human beings with OCD may additionally apprehend guilt as greater threatening than others, making it intolerable for them. Any belief or impulse that conjures up guilt may be met with intense anxiety and compulsive behavior. Importantly, this is relevant to being extremely sensitive to guilt, no longer simply being guilt-inclined.

Your starting situations

According to a 2016 take a look at published in JAMA Psychiatry, people who've been born through C-phase, preterm or breech, were particularly massive or small as infants or had a mom who smoked 10 cigarettes or more consistent with day within the route of being pregnant seem like at a better risk of growing OCD. In a take a look at of two.Four million youngsters in Sweden, about 17,000 advanced OCD, with a mean age at analysis of 23.

The researchers placed that the extra of those character factors an infant encountered, the better the hazard of developing OCD. However, this kind of have a take a look at can't show that those elements induced the OCD; it is able to handiest display that they have got been related to it. The test is however every other purpose to inspire women to cease smoking while pregnant.

Chapter 7: Treatment Options

Because this conduct exacerbates rather than relieves the character's anxiety, the obsessive thoughts and compulsive actions that outline OCD extend every other, necessitating treatment that could offer OCD symptom treatment. There are presently numerous hooked up OCD treatment alternatives, every with various ranges of efficacy and ability issue outcomes. It is recommended which you discuss together with your scientific doctor to decide the tremendous treatment for your unique symptoms and goals.

Deep TMS

Deep Transcranial Magnetic Stimulation is a unique treatment method that employs magnetic fields to securely, correctly, and non-invasively reap mind structures related to intellectual health conditions.

Deep TMS has been FDA-cleared to deal with OCD for the cause that 2018, demonstrating its ability to offer super remedy to the ones laid low with this example. This statement modified into showed by way of the usage of the usage of a 2019 multicenter, sham-controlled scientific studies look at published inside the American Journal of Psychiatry, which located Deep TMS to successfully and thoroughly alleviate OCD signs and symptoms and signs and symptoms, even among patients who had not superior sufficiently with medication or remedy.

Deep TMS is a non-invasive form of remedy that does not require anesthesia, can be included into an person's every day regular, and has no extended-time period or extensive aspect outcomes.

Cognitive conduct remedy (CBT)

CBT is a shape of speak remedy that is used as a number one-line remedy for OCD. CBT, while administered with the resource of a knowledgeable highbrow fitness professional, specializes within the thoughts, emotions, behaviors, and bodily reactions related to OCD. This is done to familiarize the affected character with the situation's diverse factors and frequently alleviate its symptoms and signs and symptoms.

Several types of treatment have developed from CBT through the years to provide sufferers with OCD with extra symptom comfort. Acceptance and strength of mind therapy (ACT) is the most awesome of these: ACT encourages openness and flexibility in reaction to OCD signs, due to the fact the therapist assists the affected man or woman in defining and carrying out a dedication to their very own properly-being.

Exposure and Response Therapy (ERP)

ERP is a shape of remedy that has been confirmed to correctly address OCD. ERP assists the affected person in overcoming OCD via grade by grade exposing them to stimuli related to OCD-inducing tension. The affected individual is usually recommended to avoid reacting to stimuli in a forced manner, and they step by step grow to be acquainted with managing OCD-associated, tension-inducing behavior.

Psychopharmacology

Medication is every specific sort of remedy this is regularly used because the first line of remedy for OCD. The FDA has permitted numerous selective serotonin reuptake inhibitors (SSRIs), along with the branded drug treatments Prozac and Zoloft, as well as one tricyclic antidepressant (TCA), to treat the condition, with SSRIs being most of the maximum regularly prescribed beauty of medicine.

Though many sufferers tormented by OCD symptoms and signs and symptoms and signs report remedy from psychopharmacology, many moreover revel in quite some element outcomes and can decide to prevent this form of treatment due to their severity.

Psychodynamic treatment has furthermore been shown to help patients with OCD. This remedy specializes within the relationships and sports that, among different factors of the affected individual's life, are essential to their enjoy of self, worldview, and personal narrative. These factors are then examined in terms of the bad OCD signs and symptoms they're experiencing, a good way to advantage a better facts of the underlying motives for how they respond to the anxiety their situation reasons. Over time, the affected character should be capable of transition a long way from routinely responding to introduced approximately anxiety and towards extra flexible, calming, and useful reactions.

Other Invasive Treatments

Despite the diverse options available to the ones suffering from OCD, a few sufferers do no longer find comfort from first-line or non-invasive OCD treatments. As a quit end result, healthcare professionals may additionally moreover provide neurosurgical alternatives to remedy-resistant patients.

Recent studies the use of numerous neurological lesion techniques have demonstrated some efficacy in lowering OCD signs and symptoms and symptoms in treatment-resistant sufferers. Gamma knife coagulative lesions, radioactive seed implants that cause community ablations, and modern day craniotomy are a number of the techniques used. Ablative neurosurgical alternatives constantly cognizance at the mind's cortico-striato-thalamo-cortical circuit, that is idea to emerge as hyperactive in patients with OCD.

In addition to the invasiveness and recuperation time required after such techniques, it ought to be noted that research analyzing those strategies are usually based totally mostly on open trials with a small range of patients. As a cease result, their efficacy inside the famous OCD population has but to be hooked up, necessitating massive, blinded studies to determine how powerful they may be in reducing OCD signs and signs and symptoms and signs and symptoms.

Tips for a Successful OCD Treatment

Here, he lists a few suggestions for a success OCD remedy:

OCD can sometimes make you doubt your homework.

It can also advocate which you aren't receiving appropriate treatment, that your assignments can't possibly beautify you, or which you genuinely do now not recognize what you're doing and will not be capable of make it artwork. Remember that OCD is referred to as the Doubting Disease, and it's going to try and stable doubt on a few element vital to you. To fight this, you could ought to take delivery of as proper with it, saying, ''Yes, it's miles accurate. "I truly won't get better."

Never forget about approximately you have OCD

This method you can not continuously be capable of receive as actual with your personal reactions or what you do not forget you studied and sense, specifically inside the event that they seem like telling you a few detail terrible and excessive. If you are uncertain whether or no longer a few component is a symptom, deal with it as such. It's better to get a bit extra exposure than no longer enough.

Remember that the problem with OCD is not tension, but compulsions

If you agree with that anxiety is the problem, you may engage in more compulsions to conquer it. If you apprehend that the compulsions are the hassle, save you sporting out them, and remain inside the apprehensive situation, the tension will in the end subside as you broaden tolerance.

Always count on the unexpected

Obsessive mind can arise at any time or in any location. Don't be amazed if antique or new ones appear. Don't allow it trouble you. Be prepared to apply your treatment device at any time and from any area. Also, if new thoughts stand up, notify your therapist that allows you to stay informed.

Be willing to take risks

Risk is an unavoidable a part of lifestyles, and consequently cannot be absolutely removed. Remember that not improving is the fine chance of all.

Never are looking for for reassurance from your self or others

Instead, tell yourself that the worst will show up, is taking vicinity, or has already came about. Reassurance will negate the effects of any remedy homework you whole and prevent you from progressing. Reassurance-searching out is a compulsion, no matter the way you justify it.

Always try to just accept as actual with all obsessive mind

Never examine, query, or argue with them. The questions they pose are not actual, and there aren't any real solutions to them. When agreeing, attempt now not to enter an excessive amount of element; really kingdom that the thoughts are actual and actual.

Don't waste time searching for to prevent or keep away from wondering your thoughts

This will most effective have the alternative effect, fundamental to more mind. Studies have demonstrated which you can't efficiently save you or suppress precise mind. "If you need to think concerning them an awful lot less, think about them extra."

Try not to anticipate in black-and-white, all-or-not something terms

Don't inform yourself that one slip-up manner you are a complete failure. If you slip and engage in a compulsion, you could typically opposite it and perform a little trouble to cancel it. The proper information is that you're in it for the prolonged haul, and you may commonly have a few other danger. It is normal to make mistakes on the equal time as getting to know new capabilities, specially in remedy. It takes area to anybody now and again. Accept it. Even if you revel in a outstanding setback, do now not allow it derail you.

Remember the pronouncing: 'A lapse is not in fact a relapse, which means that that that you could in no way in fact start over. To accomplish that, you could want to miss the whole lot you had determined out as plenty as that element, this is simply no longer feasible. Keep in thoughts the mantras, "You can constantly start over," and "Never confuse a unmarried defeat with a totally final defeat," as they are saying in AA.

Remember which you are definitely liable for managing your symptoms and symptoms

Do no longer consist of others to your remedy homework (besides your therapist instructs you to) or expect them to push or motivate you. They may not constantly be to be had whilst you need them, but you can commonly be there for your self.

Don't become impatient with your development or observe your self to others

Everyone actions at their very very very own pace. Instead, try to awareness on finishing every day's remedy homework, one after the alternative.

When given the selection, continuously choose out to stand your anxiety instead of avoid it

The high-quality manner to overcome worry (tension) is to confront it. You can't escape from your own mind, so you haven't any preference however to confront them. If you want to get better, you need to do this.

If your therapist assigns you an assignment which you do not feel organized to complete, you may talk up and permit them to apprehend.

Chapter 8: Mindfulness Practices For Ocd

Mindfulness is an innate potential that everyone people very own but won't recognize a way to use. Mindfulness is basically about being absolutely gift and conscious. This approach that even as you workout mindfulness, you apprehend that the thoughts that arise on your thoughts are not what defines you, and you are not obligated to behave on them. When you workout intentional mindfulness, you experience your mind as an observer, processing them greater deeply and severely.

You also can experience or experience your breath and frame, which allows your thoughts to lighten up and approach its surroundings. This can assist many people experience a amazing deal much less beaten or reactive, and it can specially help people with OCD in processing their thoughts about their compulsions and keeping off appearing on them.

A 2013 have a study comparing the use of mindfulness and meditation to the use of distraction in 30 OCD patients observed that those who used mindfulness talents felt a good buy lots less pressured to offer in to their compulsions, at the same time as individuals who used distraction techniques observed no alternate.

When you've got OCD, mindfulness can be particularly hard due to the truth being in the gift 2d can contain traumatic intrusive thoughts, feelings, and sensations. When you practice mindfulness, you are requested to deliberately allow the ones intrusive thoughts or feelings to exist in preference to attempting to save you them through compulsion. In this revel in, mindfulness is just like exposure and response prevention (ERP).

ERP encourages OCD sufferers to confront their triggers and combat the urge to neutralize them with compulsions. Mindfulness requires you to be conscious of intrusive mind or triggers, obtain and probably internalize any discomforts because of such mind, and withstand the urge to answer with compulsions. Both practices include taking a deeper and longer observe your preliminary reactions or thoughts and working to keep away from responding to them. This motion in mindfulness shifts your mind out of fight-or-flight mode, providing you with the time and location to clearly way, loosen up, and gain manage over your compulsions.

Ways to Practice Mindfulness

There are many unfastened assets to be had that will help you start with mindfulness techniques. Different techniques often paintings for great people; there may be no proper or wrong way to practice mindfulness, and it's miles often important to check to determine which approach is high-quality for you. Some mindfulness techniques are:

Purposeful breaks are taken in the direction of the day.

Meditations that arise at the same time as sitting, walking, or moving.

Meditation mixed with bodily interest, which include schooling yoga or sports activities sports sports.

Meditation can be specially powerful for mindfulness because it calls to be able to connect with your breath and frame, which often obviously draws you out of intrusive or cyclical thoughts. When you are targeted on sitting in the right posture and breathing deeply, your thoughts can be distracted from wandering and brought decrease returned to your connection with the frame.

Where to Practice Mindfulness

The benefit of education mindfulness is that it could be used every time and everywhere you're. If you be aware intrusive thoughts creeping in, take a 2d to take a seat down down with them and breathe. Allow the mind to be, and face up to the urge to reply to any compulsions they may elicit. You can practice this even as sitting in public, meditating by myself for your bed room, or on the grocery hold filling your cart. It honestly calls for a 2nd of stillness or the functionality to pause and take a look at your thoughts.

The most not unusual false impression about mindfulness is that it calls as a way to sit and meditate silently. This is not the case, as there are numerous strategies for incorporating mindfulness into your every day existence! You might also need to exercising mindfulness whilst running at the treadmill or taking note of your favourite album. It's all about taking the time to truely experience the existing 2d, regardless of in which you're.

Getting Started with Mindfulness

One opportunity is to meditate. A number one technique is to concentrate your attention to your very very own breathing, a workout generally referred to as ''aware breathing. After dedicating time to conscious breathing, you may locate it much less tough to interest attention for your breath in normal life, that's an important know-how for handling pressure, anxiety, and bad feelings, cooling down even as your mood flares, and sharpening your capacity to concentrate.

15 mins regular with day for as a minimum in step with week, even though research suggests that mindfulness improves with workout.

The most primary method of conscious respiratory is to pay interest your hobby to your breath, each breathing in and exhaling. You can do that fame, but it is high-quality to take a seat down down or lie down in a snug characteristic. Your eyes may be open or closed, but closing them might also moreover additionally help you interest more correctly. It can assist to time table this exercising, however it is able to moreover assist to exercising it whilst you feel specifically stressed or demanding. Experts believe that training mindful respiration on a normal basis will allow you to do higher in tough conditions.

Sometimes, mainly at the same time as trying to calm your self down in a stressful scenario, it could assist to start with an exaggerated breath: a deep inhale thru your nostril for 3 seconds, maintain your breath for at the least 2 seconds, and do a long exhale thru your mouth. Otherwise, in truth take a look at each breath without trying to alter it; it is able to be useful to pay attention at the rise and fall of your chest or the feeling thru your nose. As you achieve this, you may be aware that your thoughts wanders, distracted thru way of mind or physical sensations. That is good enough. Simply renowned that this is taking region and gently redirect your hobby once more to your breath.

Find a comfortable and cushty position

You may be sitting in a chair or at the floor with a cushion. Keep your returned without delay however no longer too tight, and your fingers relaxation anywhere they're most snug. Place your tongue at the roof of your mouth or anywhere it feels maximum snug.

Consider and lighten up your frame

Try to be aware your frame's shape and weight. Allow your self to lighten up and become curious about your frame while seated proper right here, the sensations it feels, the contact, and the connection with the ground or chair. Relax any regions which is probably tight or demanding. Just breathe.

Pay interest to how you are breathing

Feel the natural go with the flow of breath outside and inside, there may be no need to do a little thing to capture your breath. Not lengthy or short, surely natural. Consider in that you feel your breath for your complete body. It is probably to your tummy. It may be for your chest, throat, or nostrils. See if you could experience the sensations of respiratory one after the other. When one respiratory cycle ends, the subsequent one begins.

Be kind for your wandering thoughts

As you try this, you could phrase that your mind begin to wander. You may possibly find out yourself considering other things, it isn't a problem if this takes place, and it's far very herbal. Simply test that your thoughts has wandered. Say "wondering" or "wandering" for your head slowly. Then evenly redirect your hobby lower back for your respiratory.

Stay proper right right here for 6–8 minutes

Observe your breath in silence. You will on occasion turn out to be out of location in belief, only to return to your breath. Check-in in advance than you test out.

After a couple of minutes, phrase your entire body, seated right proper here. Allow yourself to lighten up even extra deeply, after which express your gratitude for doing this practice nowadays.

You also can notice that your thoughts wanders, distracted with the beneficial resource of thoughts or bodily sensations. That is ok Simply well known that that is occurring and gently redirect your interest lower once more to your breath.

It's crucial to maintain in thoughts that your cause isn't to easy your mind or preserve it from wandering. Your aim is to be completely gift in the 2d, with out judgment. Your mind can also additionally moreover wander at the same time as you parent in this, and that is best! Simply be aware about your mind and test them with out placing more pressure or judgment on yourself.

It can also seem easy, however preserve in mind that it's far called mindfulness workout for proper purpose. It does now not come sincerely to genuinely everybody, and it is surely everyday to war with it at first. To beautify, as with any muscle, intentional exercising is needed—and the strive is properly nicely well worth it.

Chapter 9: Establishing A Support System

An OCD manual system is your help device throughout your OCD treatment. These are the humans you could name at five a.M. If you're having a panic attack over the opportunity of stabbing your more younger sibling on the same time as your dad and mom are away on a corporation experience. Most importantly, they will offer you with beneficial resource.

According to researchers, humans with a healthful assist machine are much more likely to make and keep improvement than those without a healthy help gadget or no help tool in any respect. The elaborate detail about developing an OCD assist employer is that we regularly want to include individuals who do no longer completely apprehend the task for masses of reasons, together with a lack of awareness, too many stressors, their very own highbrow health troubles, and so on.

After years of operating in an OCD software program in which people stay with one of a kind people identified with OCD, I found out that this bond have end up crucial in managing OCD signs and symptoms and signs and symptoms and keeping development in treatment. Some of the relationships authentic via the ones human beings are though in location these days and are likely to thrive within the future because of the fact they keep each different responsible in a supportive manner. Building an OCD help enterprise may be hard in the beginning, however handiest you could determine whether or no longer or no longer the advantages of freedom from anxiety are really worth the effort.

Now that we recognize it is been scientifically verified that having a incredible social useful resource system can help people with OCD, it makes enjoy for everybody to get one, right? I get hold of as right with so. If you have already had been given a assist tool, I project you to assess your OCD assist to ensure that they'll be supporting you in choice to accidentally supporting your OCD.

One of the maximum not unusual errors people make at the same time as building their OCD assist community is which includes folks that lead them to demanding. If they're already worrying, and this person is going to make you even more traumatic, whether on purpose or not, they may not be the satisfactory choice. This happens frequently with own family human beings. Thus, circle of relatives remedy may be beneficial. For example, if an individual is working on their perfectionism and their guardians are prompted because of the reality their middle worry is disappointing their guardians, they may now not be the exceptional human beings to assist currently, but they are capable of become it.

Another commonplace mistake is deciding on useful aid individuals but in no way confirming whether or now not those human beings consider their newfound enterprise enterprise involvement or that OCD manual exists the least bit. When this takes location, the benefits of OCD help are in no way found out. This normally takes place due to the fact inquiring for assist can purpose tension. It's publicity time!

Individuals regularly make the mistake of failing to speak how they want to be supported within the course of tough times with their own family humans. This isn't uncommon among folks who do not completely apprehend OCD, and it could bring about by means of accident feeding the OCD in choice to gaining freedom. For example, if your buddy expresses hassle about inappropriately touching a little one, your instinct may be to say something like, "You have to in no manner try this due to the truth you're a type individual," to make her enjoy higher. However, this is probably with the aid of chance offering reassurance to the man or woman while developing the center worry.

The gain of the use of this approach is its simplicity, as there are high-quality 3 steps involved. Anticipatory anxiety may strive to steer you in any other case, but hold in mind that all of the situations you're worried approximately may not even occur, so you're stressing yourself out for not something. I assignment you to make the selection to allow yourself to enjoy uncomfortable emotions of hysteria for a quick time body in case you want to gather lifelong manual.

Steps for Assembling OCD Support.

Identify your participants.

When identifying your individuals, you have to bear in mind a few factors:

Can you be inclined around this person?

Are you involved that this individual will decide you because of the OCD?

Will this man or woman assist you in a healthful manner?

Would this arrangement motive strain inside the courting?

Potential stressful situations

Many people make the mistake of believing that their circle of relatives human beings are their primary supply of OCD help. However, in a few instances, a member of the family may not be the top notch choice due to situations which consist of OCD signs and symptoms disrupting the residence, inflicting frustration, OCD signs and symptoms disrupting own family individuals' lives, own family individuals looking to help but in reality feeding the OCD, and so on. It's a perplexing scenario due to the reality, greater frequently than not, own family contributors want their loved ones with OCD to get better extra than everybody else. It is hard to strike a balance amongst compassion and frustration; many households who have a cherished one identified with OCD require help with this.

Many human beings with OCD experience ashamed of their behaviors, and this makes it hard for them to be around own family because of the truth they sense like a burden all of the time and are afraid of being judged for their signs. Family participants, by chance, can be a direct purpose for anxiety due to emotions of shame. While this can be worked out, you may probable though require help inside the interim.

Loved ones do now not want to look every distinctive in pain. So it is secure to anticipate that during case you're experiencing prolonged anxiety because of a purpose, your loved ones will go to any duration to relieve your struggling. Whether which means coming over with a huge bath of frozen yogurt within the nighttime to make you revel in higher, lending you a shoulder to cry on, or maybe doing a little of your compulsions so one can relieve stress.

The first examples are brilliant, however a loved one want to no longer have interaction in compulsions for someone identified with OCD. This is some other motive why deciding on folks that are acquainted with OCD and function additionally lengthy long past through OCD treatment can be beneficial. They can relate to the manner you revel in due to the fact they may be also going via it and recognize how difficult it is able to be in a manner that others can not, in particular if you have similar subtypes or were in equal treatment applications.

Reach out to individuals

Shame can despite the fact that have an effect on the effectiveness of OCD remedy if it is added on via a state of affairs as opposed to a selected character. This is the disgrace that prevents us from searching for OCD help, no matter the fact that we'd probable advantage from it. If this step isn't always finished, you have had been given carried out the intellectual fitness identical of committing to mastering to run after which looking to exercise without first lacing up your shoestrings. You need that help on the way to exercise and improve.

So, what do I say once I've chosen my organization? I can't will let you recognise exactly what to mention, but because of the reality we comprehend communication is important, you could take those steps that will help you bring your message:

Share your aid desires.

Ask if they want to take part.

Determine the subsequent steps.

If they're pronouncing certain, deliver an reason for what form of help you require and affirm that they may provide it.

If no longer, recognize their needs and find out someone else.

It's honestly regular to experience hesitant. It's hard to be inclined in the front of others, even if you're near. However, maintain in mind that you are doing this to unfastened yourself from OCD, and ERP has been tested by the usage of scientists to be the only treatment. If you want extra convincing, recall what you've got attempted earlier than. Has a few component you've got attempted produced the consequences you desired? If not, it seems like it's time to strive a few element new. Consider what you may do if the jobs had been reversed and one of the human beings you chose approached you approximately something similar. When you are suffering with OCD, advantage out in your assist machine. Whatever you do, do not forget that your supporters have your decrease lower back.

Having OCD assist will increase your possibilities of managing your OCD. You assemble this assist by the usage of identifying unique human beings with whom you may be prone and accumulate healthy assist. Then touch them, devise a recreation plan precise for your desires, and located it into movement.

Chapter 10: Developing Coping Strategies

Understanding and utilising numerous coping capabilities is important for dealing with OCD. These abilities are normally categorized into 4 instructions: emotional, cognitive, social, and physical. Each category is supposed to deal with a one of a type detail of your OCD experience, and a complete technique that consists of all training can bring about more powerful control.

Emotional Coping Strategies for OCD

When OCD triggers overwhelming emotions, it's miles critical to have coping techniques. Emotional coping skills are mainly designed to assist humans stay grounded and avoid emotional spirals. Here are some confirmed emotional coping strategies for OCD:

Deep respiratory

This technique lowers your coronary coronary heart price, promotes rest, and decreases tension. It's a easy but powerful way to take control of your emotional u . S . A ..

Mindfulness

Being present within the second can assist divert your hobby some distance from OCD and reduce anxiety. This involves paying attention to the prevailing 2nd in preference to distracting thoughts.

Emotional Awareness

Recognize and famend your feelings. Don't fight them; in reality allow them to be and understand they will bypass. This popularity weakens the power of emotions.

Art treatment

Expressing your emotions through artwork can assist to lessen their intensity and offer a creative outlet for tension.

Music Therapy

Listening to or making music can also have a recuperation effect, helping to relax and distract the mind.

Cognitive Coping Skills for OCD

Because OCD is commonly described via the use of way of intrusive thoughts, cognitive coping capabilities are important. These strategies are designed that will help you advantage control of your perception styles and damage the OCD cycle. Let's test some cognitive coping abilties:

Cognitive conduct treatment (CBT)

This primarily based definitely restoration approach teaches people how to recognize and alternate their concept styles, which reduces the severity of OCD signs and symptoms and symptoms.

Mindful remark

This skills entails nonjudgmental statement of your thoughts as they arrive and circulate. Detaching yourself from your mind reduces their electricity over you.

Thought stops

This approach includes consciously announcing ''prevent'' whilst unwanted thoughts upward thrust up. It is a method of gaining control over your mind.

Reframing

This technique calls at the manner to consciously shift your attitude on intrusive mind, which facilitates to reduce their terrible effect.

Acceptance and Commitment Therapy (ACT)

This form of remedy teaches you to accept intrusive thoughts with out reacting to them, decreasing their have an impact on for your behavior.

Social Coping Strategies for OCD

Individuals with OCD also can moreover conflict with social interactions at instances. However, gaining knowledge of social coping abilities permit you to manipulate your social tension, lessen feelings of isolation, and offer a bargain-wanted help. Here are a few useful social coping capabilities:

Support corporations

These groups provide a secure vicinity to percent your reviews, have a look at from others, and sense less remoted in your warfare.

Open conversation

Being open about your OCD with trusted pals and own family contributors can assist alleviate some of the burdens you'll be wearing.

Assertiveness

Learning to specific your wishes and boundaries genuinely assist you to construct higher relationships and decrease pressure.

Conflict decision

Improving your capability to clear up disagreements can result in greater satisfactory social interactions and decrease anxiety tiers.

Physical Coping Strategies for OCD

Physical coping competencies are frequently ignored, but they play an essential function in managing OCD signs and signs. Regular physical interest can assist to alleviate tension and enhance mood. Below are some bodily coping capabilities for coping with OCD:

Regular exercising

Physical interest can substantially reduce tension and beautify mood, making it an important component of a entire OCD control approach.

Balanced healthy eating plan

A nutritious weight loss plan can improve thoughts fitness, reduce tension, and beautify temper.

Sleep hygiene

Good sleep behavior can alleviate anxiety and offer the energy required to address OCD.

Yoga

This exercise combines physical poses, mindfulness, and deep respiration to effectively reduce tension.

How OCD coping techniques work

Individuals with OCD can use coping abilties to manage their illness. They are primarily based completely on the technological know-how of cognitive-behavioral remedy (CBT), mindfulness, and different healing techniques, with each aiming to cope with a selected element of OCD.

Simply placed, those competencies assist people in gaining manage of their obsessions and compulsions, reducing anxiety, and improving their popular incredible of lifestyles. The manner of the manner those abilities paintings can be divided into three stages: reputation, response, and reinforcement.

Identify obsessions and compulsions.

The first step in the use of coping competencies for OCD is spotting the presence of obsessions and compulsions.

This degree includes distinguishing between normal issues and intrusive, obsessive thinking or compulsive behaviors. It is ready becoming privy to your thoughts and behaviors and accepting their irrational and distressing nature.

Using suitable coping talents.

Once obsessions and compulsions had been positioned, the subsequent step is to reply with appropriate coping techniques. The nature of the obsession or compulsion, further to the individual's non-public options, will decide the coping method used.

For example, a person who's overwhelmed with annoying mind may also moreover moreover use mindfulness strategies to live present and keep away from becoming ate up by using way of their obsessions. Someone suffering from compulsive conduct, as an alternative, may also lease distraction strategies to break the cycle of compulsion.

Practice and beef up coping capabilities.

The very last diploma consists of continuously operating in the direction of and reinforcing the ones competencies. This degree is important for the lengthy-term treatment of OCD. Individuals who use and provide a lift to coping capabilities on a ordinary basis can steadily lessen the electricity of obsessions and compulsions.

This degree may additionally consist of putting in a ordinary mindfulness workout, attending a guide enterprise on a everyday basis, or the usage of cognitive-behavioral techniques under the supervision of a therapist.

Other Coping Skills

We've compiled a listing of OCD coping strategies. Always keep in mind that OCD is not the fault of the person affected; it's far a medical situation, similar to a few different infection, and must be treated as such.

Avoid tablets and alcohol

Drugs on the road and illicit alcohol can in short silence obsessive mind and alleviate the pain of OCD, but regular substance abuse can fast increase. According to a observe published within the Journal of Anxiety Disorders, about 25% of human beings in search of OCD remedy furthermore meet the necessities for substance use disorder. People who growth OCD signs and signs and symptoms and signs and signs and symptoms as children or young adults regularly flip to capsules and alcohol to address their intrusive mind and worry, in advance than understanding that their signs and symptoms imply a treatable highbrow fitness sickness.

Follow your OCD treatment plan

Obsessive-compulsive disorder is a continual contamination. If you are taking prescription remedy to treat OCD signs, hold to take it as directed, even in case your intrusive thoughts seem to move away. Stopping your medicinal drug can motive unsightly bodily component effects at the facet of headaches, insomnia, and nausea, in addition to the recurrence of OCD signs and signs and signs and extended tension. Without first speakme in your medical medical doctor, in no way save you taking your medicinal drug or alter the dosage.

Greeting Your OCD

OCD can sense like an uncontrollable stress ready to pounce, similar to the monster that lived below your mattress as a toddler. Instead of treating your OCD as a faceless villain, deliver it a name and a form. Perhaps you ought to name your OCD Bully, or every different name. Whatever call you supply it, it's going to help carry your OCD out of the darkness and into the light, making it much less complicated to recognize its presence. Next, offer your OCD a form; it could range from a purple blob to a cheetah.

Keep an OCD magazine

You may additionally have visible humans keep food journals to tune what they consume every day at the same time as on a diet; an OCD magazine serves the same cause. An OCD magazine can help you preserve song of your triggers, grow to be conscious of recent ones, and determine the general united states of america of your OCD. Keep your OCD mag with you anywhere you bypass, and file what takes place once you whole a compulsion.

When you've got completed journaling for the day and take a look at through your entries, ask yourself the following questions.

Why did those situations prompt my OCD?

What need to have happened if I had now not saved my resolutions?

What proof is there that my worry of "contracting a excessive contamination and spreading it to all of us I love" should virtually come real?

Begin writing awesome pages approximately what added approximately your OCD and anxiety, and why that purpose changed into greater intrusive than correct. Write down exactly what your obsession modified into at the time, and rather than looking for reassurance from others or the net, locate it in yourself through writing down why that obsession turn out to be invalid.

You also can encompass affirmations for your mag. For example, if you're having a panic attack because of the truth you suddenly receive as authentic with you have were given reduced in size germs. Write some thing like "I am no longer that particular." I am not going to be one of the loads of thousands of those who contract it. The odds are in my want. It's difficult not to balk at the same time as you write such things as that during your magazine, but surely, in case you sense a panic attack drawing near, you could re-examine what you have written for your magazine and enjoy better. Seeing your fears written down on paper makes them feel far flung and less scary. Journaling reduces their electricity over your thoughts and actions.

Exposure and Response Prevention (ERP)

When you first start ERP, start with a first-degree purpose. Once you have faced your motive, wait 10 seconds earlier than performing for your compulsion. Gradually growth the quantity of time you spend in advance than using your compulsion until you could perform the undertaking or confront the state of affairs on the same time as now not having it. As you conquer your triggers, you may development up the OCD ladder.

Refocus your interest

If you are experiencing OCD compulsions or obsessions, or suspect you are about to expand one, try to redirect your attention an extended way from the situation. You can refocus your attention each bodily or mentally. If you continue to revel in compelled to finish your obsession after the refocusing length, strive repeating the consultation.

Physically Refocus Your Attention By:

Doing bounce jacks

Get up and stroll round.

Hum a tune.

Play with a fidget toy or particular small item.

Pet a furry animal, like your cat or dog.

Mentally Refocus Your Attention By:

List the entirety you notice.

Name all of the shades you could currently think about.

Spell your call or your friend's names backward.

Say the alphabet backward.

Recite the lyrics out of your preferred tune.

Reward Yourself For Success.

While you're on foot to conquer your OCD, make time to rejoice your accomplishments. Fighting OCD is tough, so fulfillment need to be celebrated like some specific achievement. Determine your rewards in advance than hard your self. For example, you may determine that if you can wait 20 seconds earlier than completing your compulsion, you'll order pizza for dinner! You do now not want to have rewards or set expectations for each state of affairs, as this will increase strain. Perhaps on the surrender of the week, you could reward yourself for any development you've got made, or if you decide to confront a compulsion head-on, reward your self proper away. You are liable for setting the first-class balance.

Keep busy

If you aren't actively appealing your brain and body, intrusive mind are more likely to go into and occupy thoughts vicinity. Deliberate planning of sports, which consist of pastimes, artwork, domestic projects, and time with pals and circle of relatives, permit you to live targeted in a few unspecified time inside the future of the day. Simply doing different obligations allows to divert your interest faraway from obsessions and compulsions. You do now not want to plan each minute of your day, but a free time desk of activities can beautify your ordinary super of lifestyles.

Keep Stress at a Minimum

Living with and combating OCD is tough artwork, this is exacerbated thru stress. Stress has been examined to noticeably boom OCD in humans, so coping with your stress ranges is important. Include stress-relieving activities for your every day time table. Whether you drift for a run, have a look at a e-book, or watch TV, putting apart an hour every day to de-pressure can be fantastically beneficial.

Remind yourself of the facts

It is easy to fall right into a cycle of self-doubt and blame, but strive to break it. If you begin to sense accountable about having OCD, remind yourself that you have a recognized medical state of affairs. Would you be irritated at your asthmatic buddy if he had to save you and use his inhaler? Of path no longer, so you don't need to revel in lousy in case you act out of the normal or reason a minor put off. You have a systematic situation and are dealing with it. There is no want for guilt at the give up of the story.

Struggling to exercise the competencies continuously.

It may be difficult to maintain consistency in practicing OCD coping abilities, particularly inside the path of stressful conditions. Here are a few strategies to overcoming this mission.

Establish a routine

Having a tough and speedy ordinary let you exercise your coping talents greater constantly.

Involve the resource community

Sharing your desires with supportive buddies and circle of relatives can assist keep you inspired.

Use apps or reminders

Technology will will let you bear in mind to exercising your abilties each day.

Fear of not having effective coping abilities for OCD

It is natural to be worried about the efficacy of OCD coping abilties, mainly at the equal time as first starting out. Here's the way to cope with this OCD fear:

Maintain sensible expectancies

These skills aren't a short repair, but rather a part of ongoing control.

Track your development

Keeping a mag of your observations and upgrades will will can help you see the modifications over time.

Seek expert help

A intellectual health expert can reassure and guide you through your concerns and fears.

Difficulty recognizing intrusive thoughts

One of the maximum tough elements of working towards OCD coping capabilities is acknowledging intrusive mind in place of trying to suppress them. Here's the way to navigate this:

Normalize intrusive thoughts

Understand that everyone memories intrusive mind sometimes. OCD is described via the overemphasis on those thoughts.

Practice mindfulness

Mindfulness bodily video games can teach you to just accept those mind without judgment or fear.

Seek professional guidance

Therapists can educate you Cognitive-Behavioral Therapy techniques like Exposure and Response Prevention (ERP) to help you end up extra cushty with intrusive mind.

Navigating the complexities of OCD is a adventure, however with the right coping skills and expertise, its miles potential. Embracing attempted-and-right techniques and losing misconceptions can result in large improvements in mental health. If you or someone you apprehend is struggling with OCD, do not hesitate to are looking for professional assist and rely upon to be had property; your highbrow health is essential.

Chapter 11: Understanding Ocd Patterns

Gaining control and selling change in the complicated international of obsessive-compulsive sickness (OCD) calls for an attention of the patterns guiding one's thoughts and actions. The complicated styles illustrate the complexity of OCD, necessitating a more thorough investigation and a complicated method to release the sickness from the person.

Repetitive actions or mental sports activities (compulsions) completed in reaction to undesired, persistent thoughts (obsessions) are commonplace developments of OCD. This behavior trade into a vicious cycle that complements itself, producing a tough-to-harm remarks loop. Investigating the twin nature of obsessions and compulsions and their interactions is vital to records the center of OCD patterns.

OCD is basically characterized with the useful resource of the usage of everyday, disturbing mind, mind, or goals which can be called obsessions. These invasive intellectual phenomena might also take many specific shapes, which include a name for for symmetry or exactness, a fear of contamination, or a dread of hurting exceptional people. Recognizing the irrationality of those obsessions and the misery they purpose—misery this is regularly out of percent to any real-lifestyles danger—is vital to information them.

Contrarily, compulsions are movements or mind achieved in an try to ease the ache added on with the resource of obsessions. Washing, checking, counting, or repeating outstanding acts are examples of commonplace compulsions. Compulsions can also moreover provide quick-term solace, but in the long run, they perpetuate the obsession-compulsion cycle and add to the sickness's staying strength.

A vicious cycle of obsession and compulsion is produced thru their interaction. Anxiety or soreness brought on with the useful resource of obsessions stress people to do compulsions in an try and offset or reduce these undesirable feelings. Ironically, the obsessive-compulsive cycle gets more installed the extra compulsions are finished, strengthening the patterns that outline the situation.

It is vital to become aware of the underlying cognitive distortions that underlie OCD as a manner to recognize those styles well. Common cognitive distortions linked to OCD embody overestimating chance, being illiberal of ambiguity, and engaging in catastrophic wondering. In order to interrupt the loop of compulsive behaviors, it's miles essential to project the illogical ideas that underlie obsessions so that you can get to the bottom of these distortions.

The evaluation and comprehension of those patterns is drastically aided thru recovery modalities like cognitive-behavioral treatment (CBT). In cognitive behavioral treatment (CBT), patients and a therapist collaborate to apprehend, question, and reframe defective wondering strategies. This manner attempts to interrupt the obsessive behaviors that feed the OCD cycle in addition to addressing the intense struggling delivered on via obsessions.

Furthermore, comprehending the complex forms of OCD calls for investigating the triggers that set off obsessions and the following compulsions. Individual versions can be seen in triggers, which can in all likelihood have their origins particularly occasions, mind, or emotional states. Identifying those triggers helps human beings understand the context of their OCD behaviors, which makes it simpler to apply focused therapeutic techniques.

It's moreover important to recognize the time detail of OCD patterns. OCD signs and symptoms and signs regularly variety in reaction to stress, changes in lifestyles, or different out of doors variables. Understanding the dynamic nature of these styles lets in humans to better manipulate the united statesand downs in their OCD symptoms, expect barriers, and placed proactive coping mechanisms into exercising.

Peeling lower lower again the layers of compulsions, obsessions, and cognitive distortions to find out the complicated systems that guide the circumstance is essentially the gadget of comprehending OCD styles. It requires a aggregate of treatment intervention, introspection, and a energy of mind to confronting and enhancing unhelpful highbrow conduct. With this know-how, human beings set out on a avenue to free up themselves from the cyclical pattern of OCD, growing a lifestyles this is in the long run characterised by way of peace in preference to obsession.

The Value of Calm in Coping with OCD

The quest of calmness becomes a critical cornerstone within the recuperation method from the complicated terrain of obsessive-compulsive disease (OCD). The importance of developing serenity and tranquility is going past emotional fitness; it turns into a powerful stimulant for escaping the entangling keep of the obsessive thoughts and compulsive actions that outline OCD. This studies explores the severa sides of tranquility, revealing its massive importance in conquering OCD and cultivating a resilient, balanced lifestyles.

Fundamentally, serenity refers to a scenario of inner calm and quiet, a haven amid the turbulent global of mental fitness. The relentless onslaught of intrusive thoughts and the obsessive behaviors that accompany them can also additionally reason a chronic undercurrent of fear and distress in human beings with OCD. The rate of tranquility in this case comes from its ability to counteract the turbulence of OCD thru appearing as an antidote.

A primary obstacle supplied via using manner of OCD is the exaggeration of not unusual stimuli into abnormally excessive tiers of worry. Therefore, tranquility acts as a barrier within the direction of this heightened emotional response. People can also additionally reduce the effect of obsessive thoughts and destroy the cycle of compulsion that commonly follows via developing a mentality that values tranquility.

Developing a practical and intentional highbrow alternate is frequently crucial on the path to tranquility. In order to anchor oneself inside the present second, mindfulness strategies are important to this system. By encouraging humans to be aware their mind without passing judgment, mindfulness enables humans increase an focus which can intrude with the automatic and frightening responses which might be everyday of OCD.

Furthermore, tranquility balances out the turmoil that intrusive mind may additionally carry into normal lifestyles. Finding serenity within the midst of intrusive mind is a popularity that one can also coexist quietly with the ones mind without giving in to their goals, now not a denial of the issues provided through OCD.

Therapeutic strategies for OCD remedy often pressure how vital it's miles to installation coping techniques that sell tranquility. An set up and a success treatment for OCD, cognitive-behavioral remedy (CBT), has additives that deal with the behavioral sorts of compulsions in addition to the cognitive distortions that underlie obsessions. CBT goals to installation a highbrow surroundings that is favorable to peace through the use of manner of questioning illogical mind and converting maladaptive behavior.

The exercising of cultivating peace goes past restoration processes and encompass way of life adjustments. A entire technique for resolving OCD consists of growing physical activities that emphasize self-care, embracing strain-relieving sports activities sports, and growing a supportive surroundings. These adjustments in way of residing not terrific right away contribute to calmness but provide the foundation for lengthy-time period nicely-being.

Crucially, tranquility is the ability to face difficulties head-on with poise and fortitude rather than the absence of issues. Keeping one's composure calls for accepting that setbacks are an inevitable part of the recuperation approach. When confronted with limitations, human beings may additionally additionally rely on their developed revel in of composure to deal with problems with readability and unwavering will to maintain going.

Since the consequences of OCD are not restrained to the person who is experiencing it, the concept of tranquility also applies to interpersonal interactions. Family individuals are often pretty vital in offering encouragement, expertise, and aid. Through encouraging candid communication and enlightening others of their immediate place about the individual of OCD, human beings may additionally moreover installation a community of manual that helps they all experience comfortable in the large scheme of factors.

Moreover, finding tranquility is a non-prevent technique that calls for willpower and flexibility. It includes developing a self-control to self-discovery, figuring out the specific factors that contribute to absolutely everyone's properly-being, and adjusting strategies effectively. This individualized technique emphasizes the charge of accepting specialty within the technique of recuperation through the use of acknowledging that what gives tranquility to at least one individual won't be the same for some other.

In precis, peace of thoughts is crucial for conquering OCD in lots of unique techniques. It acts as a stimulus for escaping the compulsive loop, a buffer in opposition to exaggerated emotional reactions, and a evaluation to the scary individual of obsessive thoughts. People can also take a transforming adventure within the path of inner peace thru the usage of mindfulness strategies, recovery remedies, and way of existence changes.

Instead of being an now not possible excellent, serenity emerges as a concrete and effective force—a beacon of hope for a existence marked with the useful resource of equilibrium, fortitude, and long-lasting healing from OCD.

Chapter 12: Recognizing Individual Triggers

Deciphering the complex network of compulsive movements and obsessive mind that make up obsessive-compulsive disorder (OCD) calls for first recognizing personal triggers these triggers, which might be regularly precise to absolutely everyone, characteristic initiators of the horrifying pattern that characterizes OCD Determining and identifying the ones triggers lays the muse for focused treatment options and prolonged-term rehabilitation while additionally illuminating the underlying reasons of obsessions and compulsions.

When it involves OCD, private triggers also can take many exclusive forms. They might be particular sports, thoughts, feelings, or possibly tactile sensations. Identifying the ones triggers requires a higher diploma of self-attention, a readiness to find out the internal workings of one's very very very own thoughts, and an data that going via ache head-on is a necessary step at the direction to recovery.

Situational instances are one kind of purpose that is frequently encountered. Obsessive mind may additionally moreover thrive in superb conditions and locations, which can bring about extended tension and the want for obsessive sports activities. For example, an individual suffering from infection-related obsessions should find out that being in busy or public areas triggers their want to smooth their hands plenty. Recognizing those times serves as a basis for growing specialised techniques to effectively control the ones triggers.

Another essential class is idea triggers, which is probably characterized thru the use of certain cognitive techniques that elicit compulsive thoughts. These might be unreasonable doubts, dire forecasts, or irrational issues. People might probable begin to recognize the cognitive distortions underlying their obsessions with the useful resource of attentively investigating the topics and substance of these mind. By using techniques like cognitive-behavioral treatment (CBT), humans may moreover moreover damage the obsessive-compulsive cycle thru analyzing to impeach and reframe the ones faulty wondering techniques.

OCD and emotional triggers are intently related on the grounds that obsessions may additionally furthermore have a more impact whilst an person is experiencing progressed emotions. Anxiety, despair, stress, or perhaps pride may also moreover moreover function triggers, escalating compulsive behaviors and obsessive mind. By spotting the emotional surroundings that surrounds OCD episodes, human beings can also additionally create targeted coping mechanisms, such mindfulness sporting occasions or relaxation techniques, to address these triggers greater skillfully.

Furthermore, OCD may be introduced about by means of the use of using sensory cues.

Some tactile stories, visible cues, or aural alerts can also activate compulsive mind and behaviors. Knowing those sensory triggers allows humans to adjust their environment or participate in sensory-focused treatment as part of a holistic approach for controlling OCD.

Finding one's non-public triggers often involves a combination of statement, introspection, and running with highbrow fitness specialists. It can be very helpful to maintain an intensive pocket e book of compulsive moves, obsessive mind, and the conditions that surround them. Through the act of retaining a diary, people also can see tendencies over the years that result in a more recognition in their personal triggers and the functionality to make properly-knowledgeable picks at some point in their restoration.

Working with a highbrow health professional, such an OCD-expert therapist, offers some other stage of records to the device of pinpointing triggers. Through focused inquiry, therapists assist customers in finding connections and patterns that might not be right away obvious. Through this cooperative attempt, human beings can also additionally study their triggers in a judgment-free, supportive and knowledgeable environment.

Once identified, character triggers serve as the middle of attention for therapeutic techniques. A key element of CBT for OCD is exposure and response prevention (ERP), which includes introducing human beings to their triggers regularly whilst discouraging them from taking component in obsessive behaviors. With the assist of this methodical technique, human beings may additionally additionally reduce their tension, growth their resilience, and ultimately surrender the cycle of compulsion.

A complex a part of handling OCD is customizing coping mechanisms to specific triggers. For example, if a person has a phobia of contamination, they may try to grade by grade reveal themselves to situations that reason it at the same time as overcoming the need to easy masses. Similar to this, those who have a need to test need to paintings on controlling their impulse to test while splendid stimuli rise up.

Finding triggers requires ordinary research rather than a one-time effort. New triggers might also moreover seem or old triggers may moreover furthermore alternate as humans do better of their recovery. Keeping coping mechanisms bendy and responsive to those shifts is a key element of prolonged-time period OCD control.

In precis, step one inside the complex approach of conquering OCD is spotting one's personal triggers. It includes delving deeply into the one-of-a-kind capabilities of one's very very own psyche, seeing dispositions, and running with intellectual health experts. By being aware about and addressing those triggers, humans open the door to targeted recovery methods and offer themselves the tools they need to escape the grip of obsessive-compulsive behaviors and take steps towards living a more independent and resilient lifestyles.

Methods of Mindfulness for Peaceful Living

Mindfulness strategies have emerge as extra useful devices inside the combat towards obsessive-compulsive ailment (OCD) and within the attempting to find of peace of thoughts. They offer a street to intellectual health and internal tranquility. Originating from historical contemplative practices, mindfulness includes developing an acute interest of the cutting-edge second with out passing judgment. This research explores the extremely good effects of mindfulness on improving from OCD, explains the nuances of its strategies, and emphasizes how transformational they can be in promoting calm.

Being truely present, being attentive to the prevailing, and noting thoughts and emotions with out getting caught up in them are the critical additives of mindfulness. Mindfulness acts as an anchor to counteract the automated and unpleasant responses which can be ordinary of OCD in individuals who battle with it, a mental panorama usually dominated thru intrusive mind and compulsive behaviors.

Mindful respiration is a primary thing of mindfulness. Focusing on one's breath is a easy however powerful approach that permits people ground themselves inside the here and now. Mindful breathing turns into a grounding technique inside the placing of OCD, even as thoughts might also additionally rush and tension may increase, selling a sense of balance and presenting a secure haven from the storm of obsessive mind.

Another vital detail is conscious remark, this is having an goal recognition of mind and emotions. Mindful observers watch those intellectual activities objectively in region of hastily responding to obsessive mind or appearing compulsive actions. In order to break out the cycle of obsessions and compulsions, it is critical to boom a mentality that permits mind to go back and pass without being fed on with the useful resource of them. This is what this workout does.

The use of mindfulness practices for OCD requires the exercising of aware reputation. Acceptance includes spotting and letting cross of the need to repress or regulate one's mind and emotions. Mindful popularity turns into a modern alternate in the putting of OCD, in which the want for manipulate is often a the use of stress—a readiness to abide with ache and uncertainty without giving in to compulsions.

Dr. Jon Kabat-Zinn created the installed application referred to as mindfulness-based totally absolutely pressure discount (MBSR), which incorporates mindfulness techniques into an all-encompassing approach for strain control and properly being enhancement. MBSR creates a complete framework that treats each the physical and mental factors of nicely-being with the aid of manner of the use of frame test sports activities, guided mindfulness meditations, and mild yoga. Studies have proven that MBSR is strong in decreasing anxiety and improving OCD patients' signs and signs and symptoms.

Another adaption of mindfulness sports sports is referred to as Mindfulness-Based Cognitive Therapy (MBCT), which blends cognitive-behavioral remedy tenets with mindfulness practices. The necessities of MBCT may be used inside the setting of OCD, and it has confirmed efficacy in reducing the recurrence of depressive episodes. People who combine mindfulness into cognitive-behavioral techniques research to relate to their mind and feelings in a greater adaptable and sympathetic manner.

The flexibility of mindfulness to evolve to specific conditions and life is one in every of its benefits. It is feasible to encompass informal mindfulness strategies into normal obligations. Daily sports like consuming, on foot, and dishwashing end up probabilities to practice mindfulness. The activity's sensory experience becomes the number one emphasis, helping humans become extra mindfully privy to their environment and all of the way all the way down to earth in the gift.

The advantages of training mindfulness skip beyond the short time period. Consistent use of mindfulness practices alters the neural connections within the brain, encouraging neuroplasticity and improving emotional manipulate. The overarching goal of breaking free from OCD conduct and developing a greater adaptive coping mechanism for intrusive thoughts is in step with this neurobiological change.

Mindfulness practices are a useful adjunct to conventional treatment treatments inside the remedy of OCD. Cognitive-behavioral treatment for OCD (CBT-OCD) also can without problem encompass mindfulness, giving sufferers a big sort of gadget to successfully manage their symptoms. By together with mindfulness strategies, people can also react to obsessive mind with greater resilience and serenity because they come to be more privy to their thoughts and emotions.

Rather than requiring a total disengagement from mind or feelings, mindfulness encourages a alternate in how one interacts with them. It encourages people to approach their inner sensations with hobby and without passing judgment. This alternate in factor of view may be progressive within the putting of OCD, wherein intrusive thoughts are often accompanied thru judgment and self-grievance. It fosters self-compassion and lessens the emotional fee of the intrusive thoughts.

Chapter 13: Cognitive-Behavioral Techniques

One of the mainstays of the treatment options for treating obsessive-compulsive illness (OCD) is cognitive-behavioral therapy (CBT). With its foundation in the idea that thoughts, emotions, and moves are interrelated, cognitive behavioral therapy (CBT) gives a methodical, empirically supported manner to break the obsessive-compulsive pattern. This research explores the critical mind of cognitive-behavioral techniques, supplying perception into how they may be used within the context of OCD and the ability transformation they offer in overcoming the styles that define the scenario.

Recognizing the Cognitive Elements:

The cognitive a part of CBT is figuring out and correcting faulty wondering procedures that underpin OCD's compulsive concept styles. Cognitive distortions along with catastrophic thinking, overestimating threat, and intolerance for ambiguity are common amongst OCD sufferers. People can also see how illogical their obsessions are via investigating the substance and veracity of those thoughts.

Cognitive Restructuring: A crucial step on this method is cognitive restructuring. It entails methodically disproving and rephrasing illogical thoughts. For example, in a cognitive restructuring workout, one can also task the idea that touching a doorknob would possibly bring about disastrous repercussions if the individual has an obsession over infection. People start to undermine the idea in their obsessions when they begin to doubt the veracity of those thoughts.

The Conducting Elements:

Breaking the loop of compulsive actions that come after obsessive thoughts is the number one purpose of CBT's behavioral difficulty. One of the maximum vital behavioral techniques inside the treatment of OCD is publicity and reaction prevention, or ERP.

Exposure and Response Prevention (ERP): ERP is methodically exposing people to times that set off their obsessions as a way to forestall the subsequent compulsive reaction. A character who fears infection, for example, can an increasing number of face instances in which they enjoy contaminated and keep away from doing ritualistic cleansing. Through this publicity, humans are capable of face their concerns, enjoy soreness with out the obsessive coping mechanism, and subsequently find out that their worst concerns are unfounded.

Combining Behavioral and Cognitive Elements:

CBT's energy is its capability to integrate behavioral and cognitive techniques even as acknowledging the complex courting that exists among OCD sufferers' thoughts and behaviors. Therapy-delivered approximately cognitive restructuring works to refute and regulate the false mind that underpin obsessions. Behavioral treatments simultaneously interfere with the styles of compulsive responses, decreasing the grip of the obsessive-compulsive cycle.

CBT with mindfulness:

With the developing integration of mindfulness practices into CBT for OCD, humans now have a similarly device to help them cope with intrusive thoughts. By encouraging humans to examine their thoughts with out passing judgment, mindfulness promotes a non-reactive mind-set closer to obsessions. This mindfulness exercise improves the cognitive flexibility required to question and reinterpret illogical thoughts.

Creating Coping Mechanisms:

CBT gives sufferers useful coping mechanisms they may use outside of treatment. These strategies include of assertiveness schooling, relaxation strategies, and trouble-solving abilities. People end up better at navigating barriers each within and out of doors of remedy intervals via using building a severa arsenal of coping strategies.

CBT's Collaborative Character:

Because cognitive behavioral remedy (CBT) is essentially collaborative, therapists collaborate with customers to customize remedy plans to satisfy their unique desires and limitations. A feeling of empowerment and ownership over the recovery way is fostered with the resource of this collaborative element.

Assignments for Homework and Developing Skills:

Individuals present approach CBT frequently have homework to do in amongst training. These obligations provide the risk to growth new abilties and comply with strategies received in treatment to practical settings. Long-lasting exchange is facilitated with the aid of normal exercising, which enhances new behavioral and cognitive styles.

Examining Fundamental Beliefs:

CBT explores the evaluation of center ideals, which may be ingrained, often unconscious perspectives about oneself, the out of doors worldwide, and one's own destiny. These vital mind resource the staying strength of OCD signs and signs and symptoms. Those who understand and confront the ones ideas are better capable of recognize the underlying reasons of their obsessive-compulsive behaviors.

Gradual Development and Relapse Avoidance:

CBT places a strong emphasis on stopping relapses and recognizes the cost of regular development. People can also little by little benefit manage over their thoughts and moves because of the fact to CBT's step-by means of the use of manner of-step approach. Therapists collaborate with customers to foresee destiny boundaries and create prolonged-time period maintenance plans for improvements.

Tailored and Adaptable:

CBT is an approachable, bendy approach that can be custom designed to satisfy every body's necessities. It acknowledges that individualized know-how of absolutely everyone's particular struggles and research is crucial for a success remedy. This customized method presents to CBT's efficacy in treating masses of OCD manifestations.

To sum up, cognitive-behavioral techniques offer an intensive and sensible technique of treating obsessive-compulsive sickness. Individuals participate in a transformational approach that challenges inaccurate beliefs, breaks compulsive sporting events, and supports sustainable trade via the use of the use of treating both the cognitive and behavioral additives of the circumstance. Because CBT is individualized and collaborative, it lets in people to actively take part of their personal healing, which sooner or later ends in a liberation from the grip of OCD and the restoration of a resilient and balanced life.

Chapter 14: Establishing A Network Of Support

Developing a sturdy assist network is vital to beating obsessive-compulsive disorder (OCD). Although private fortitude is important, the collective electricity of a manual device may furthermore provide valuable motivation, comprehension, and beneficial assist. This research dives into the importance of making a useful resource community, the vital components that make it paintings, and the game-changing results it may have on the street to restoration.

Understanding the Value of Assistance:

People with OCD regularly warfare in quiet with their intrusive mind and compulsions, which can be alienating A help network is form of a lifeline, presenting a feel of expertise and connection this is important for overcoming the limits that the circumstance offers. Acknowledging the rate of assist, people set out on a route that lessens the load of OCD and lays the basis for prolonged-time period nicely-being.

Support Types:

1. Relatives and Friends:The first humans to offer help are frequently near friends and partner and youngsters. Their comprehension and compassion create a type surroundings in which humans are welcomed and encouraged.

An vital first step is educating pals and own family about OCD. A more degree of recognition encourages empathy and gives cherished ones the records they need to provide useful help.

2. Therapeutic Support:Seeking professional assistance, such counseling, is important to placing collectively a entire help network. OCD-focused therapists offer path and resources for symptom control, whether or now not thru cognitive-behavioral remedy (CBT) or one in every of a kind research-primarily based strategies.

A specific dynamic is created with the beneficial aid of organization remedy or beneficial resource agencies, which lets in humans with OCD to have interaction, exchange reminiscences, and benefit information from each other. This mutual information promotes a sense of network and lessens feelings of loneliness.

3. Online groups:Online forums and corporations dedicated to OCD provide a area for humans to interact with others going via similar struggles. Online structures' anonymity is probably particularly beneficial for those who might be reluctant to talk about their recollections in public.

Components of a Successful Support Network:

1. Empathy and Understanding:Empathy and statistics are the cornerstones of a beneficial surroundings. People who get hold of the effects of OCD without passing judgment on them are helpful to people who undergo with the contamination.

People also can percentage their thoughts and feelings without traumatic approximately being judged once they talk brazenly, which creates a culture wherein data can develop.

2. Education:The foundation of green help is training. Encouraging information of OCD, its signs and symptoms and signs, and its remedy techniques makes it less complicated for aid networks to provide powerful assist.

Supporters can better customize their help on the equal time as they will be privy to the particular triggers and problems that the OCD victim faces.

three. Validation and Encouragement:Two vital additives of a assist machine are validation and encouragement. Encouraging any shape of achievement permits someone conquer OCD because it offers them self assurance.

Giving the person's studies validity enables them enjoy lots much less ashamed or insecure approximately themselves.

four. Active Participation in Treatment:Supporters can also make a proactive contribution with the resource of actively enticing with the individual's remedy method. A strength of will to the restoration process can be proven inside the crowning glory of prescribed sports, comprehension of remedy targets, and attendance at therapy durations.

Participation in remedy encourages teamwork and reinforces the concept that beating OCD calls for cooperation from all occasions.

five. Adaptability and Flexibility:OCD signs and symptoms may also moreover trade over time, and the tactics that paintings satisfactory also can. Continuous resilience can be strengthened by way of manner of a responsive, bendy, and adaptive beneficial resource tool that can regulate to changing necessities.

6. Patience:When conquering OCD, staying power is a specific characteristic. Patient supporters are conscious that restoration is a

dynamic approach, that development can be sluggish, and that setbacks would possibly in all likelihood take location.

Doable Strategies for Creating a Support Network:

1. Open Communication:Encourage candid and open communicate among human beings of the help device. Provide a constant region for the OCD victim to talk their needs, anxieties, and victories.

2. Educational Resources:Provide your pals and family with instructional substances on OCD. Books, articles, or movies can also debunk common misconceptions about the condition and offer insightful information.

three. Involvement in remedyTry to consist of circle of relatives people in treatment instructions. By taking into consideration shared intention-setting and enhancing comprehension, this inclusion reinforces the collaborative issue of treatment.

4. Support Group Participation:Promote becoming a member of on-line boards or assist companies. Developing relationships with others who have long gone through comparable matters allows people sense lots an awful lot much less by myself and greater like a part of the community.

five. Respect Boundaries:Honor the boundaries set via way of anyone. Acknowledge that they may every now and then need area or sure resorts, and look at their wishes as it have to be.

6. Celebrate Milestones:Honor great anniversaries and accomplishments all through the recovery system. Recognizing accomplishments in remedy, which incorporates reaching a reason or conquering a fear, facilitates to maintain optimism.

The Impact of Transformation:

A robust help community may additionally notably adjust the manner of overcoming OCD. The resource network's collective information lessens feelings of loneliness and acts as a protect in opposition to the emotional troubles that frequently accompany the contamination. Having the statistics that one is not the super one handling OCD promotes resilience and a sense of community.

Support networks help human beings stick with their treatments more constantly due to the truth they cause them to experience advocated and supported through way of those spherical them. The cooperative form of the assist corporation fosters a sense of agency empowerment through reaffirming the concept that beating OCD is a group attempt.

Moreover, the highbrow and pragmatic aid furnished via a help community amplifies the person's ability to manipulate everyday obstacles. The guide system contributes extensively to the character's coping mechanisms, from actively wearing out publicity bodily sports activities to lending a sympathetic ear at some stage in trying instances.

To sum up, growing a sturdy beneficial useful resource network is essential to the restoration approach from obsessive-compulsive illness. By technique of comprehension, compassion, and engaged involvement, advocates make contributions to a putting that cultivates adaptability and encourages favorable outcomes.

A sturdy manual network may additionally moreover moreover have a lifestyles-converting effect this is going beyond the character, serving as a network of individuals who are devoted to helping each other triumph over the rules of OCD and serving as a delivery of data, encouragement, and steadfast help.

Chapter 15: Modifications To Lifestyle For Calm Living

Making modifications to at the least one's lifestyle is important to selling a peaceful way of life, specifically for the ones overcoming the issues related to obsessive-compulsive sickness (OCD). Creating a manner of existence that places highbrow fitness first is a large part of the complex gadget of controlling OCD. It allows you discover your stability and calm. This study explores the crucial way of life changes that might encourage calm living and beautify the overall nicely-being of people with OCD.

Creating Healthful Habits:

1. Regular Sleep Schedules: Make sticking to a ordinary sleep pattern a concern. Regular sleep patterns lessen the risk of increased anxiety associated with erratic sleep, helping resilience and intellectual fitness.

2. Organized Daily Schedule: Creating a regimented day by day time desk ought to possibly assist offer a feel of predictability. A

pressure-unfastened, properly-planned day can also assist one enjoy emotionally extra robust.

3. Balanced Nutrition:Eating a well-balanced weight loss plan has a amazing impact on highbrow fitness. Maintaining a healthy weight loss plan promotes emotional stability and desired nicely-being.

Including Activities That Reduce Stress:

1. Physical Exercise:Engaging in everyday bodily hobby may also additionally considerably reduce strain. Exercises that enhance physical health, collectively with yoga, strolling, and walking, additionally enhance intellectual clarity and relaxation.

2. Mindfulness Practices:Include mindfulness carrying sports into your everyday ordinary. Mindfulness-based strategies which consist of respiration wearing sports, meditation, and aware walking also can help people in developing a peaceful and gift-focused mindset.

3. Artistic Expression:Use your inventive endeavors as a manner to carry who you're. Creative pursuits, which include writing, drawing, or gambling an tool, offer human beings a manner to express their emotions and sell serenity of mind.

Promoting a Helpful Environment:

1. Open conversation:Foster honest and open verbal exchange with loved ones. Understanding and empathy are fostered in a supportive environment even as humans are loose to precise their reviews and feelings without worrying about being judged.

2. Create Safe Spaces:Set aside areas in your home in that you enjoy stable and relaxed. Having a physical region that may be used as a getaway is probably specially beneficial even as anxiety is going for walks excessive.

Adopting Conscientious Technology Use:

1. Digital Detox:Conduct intermittent fasts from virtual media. Taking breaks from continuous connectivity lowers the capacity

pressure related to ongoing digital engagement and promotes highbrow renewal.

2. Mindful Social Media Use:Use social media with reputation. A greater tranquil digital revel in can be done with the aid of proscribing show time and being careful approximately the stuff one consumes.

Making Self-Care a Priority:

1. Scheduled pauses:Include planned pauses for your every day time table. A little walk, a while spent respiratory deeply, or just taking a smash from art work are all useful to preferred nicely being.

2. Restorative Activities:Take element in fun and soothing sports. Setting aside time for restorative interests like analyzing, being attentive to tune, or going out of doors promotes a calmer manner of dwelling.

Determining Limits:

1. Learn to Say No: – Get cushty establishing limits and understand even as to refuse requests. In order to stay a more balanced and stress-loose lifestyles, one need to keep away from overcommitting and appreciate one's very very personal obstacles.

2. Work-Life BalanceMake an try and keep a terrific paintings-lifestyles stability. Make time for relationships, pastimes, and self-care a scenario so that you can save you burnout and preserve brand new well being.

Establishing a Helpful Social Network:

1. Quality connections:Develop connections of satisfactory. Having a being worried and empathetic employer of humans round oneself permits one sense less on my own and further like they belong.

2. Teach Family and Friends:Inform own family individuals and pals about OCD. Raising recognition encourages empathy and creates a installing which people with OCD experience famous and understood.

Pursuing Interests That Have Meaning:

1. Survive Passions:Choose and engage in pleasing pastimes. Taking element in happy and pleasing sports activities is useful to at least one's intellectual fitness.

2. Learning and Growth:Encourage an attitude of ongoing schooling and improvement. Establishing desires and responsibilities for oneself gives one path and enhances dwelling brilliant.

Seeking Expert Assistance:

1. Therapeutic Intervention:Take below interest acquiring therapeutic help. CBT and other evidence-based totally strategies may moreover offer people the abilties and techniques they need to control their OCD symptoms and decorate their trendy outstanding of existence.

2. Medication Management:Look into medicinal drug control if a scientific expert indicates it. Medication also can occasionally be used at the facet of therapy treatment

plans and way of life modifications to assist control OCD signs.

Observing and Modifying:

1. Regular Self-Reflection:Practice self-mirrored photograph on a everyday foundation. Continuous variant and development are made viable thru keeping a watch fixed on one's emotional health and comparing the effects of lifestyle adjustments.

2. Strategy Flexibility:Exercise flexibility at the identical time as placing strategies into movement. Realize that everybody's requirements and instances are specific, and that modifying way of existence picks according with those changes promotes prolonged-term nicely-being.

Changes in manner of lifestyles characteristic the allows for intellectual and emotional health in the quest for a comfortable existence. In addition to assisting with symptom control, those changes help OCD sufferers establish the muse for a happy, healthy life. In spite of the problems posed through way of OCD, humans may additionally increase a manner of lifestyles that promotes resilience, serenity, and a sense of pleasure by using way of implementing stress-relieving sports activities, supportive surroundings, and self-care sporting events.

Chapter 16: Setting Objectives For The Recovery Of Ocd

Setting goals is a strategic and strong tool inside the remedy of obsessive-compulsive sickness (OCD). Establishing viable goals offers human beings a route ahead, encourages them to take part actively in their rehabilitation, and gives them a sense of direction. This research explores the characteristic that purpose-placing performs in OCD treatment, offers essential tips for a fulfillment purpose-setting, and highlights the game-converting ability of sincerely defined goals within the combat in opposition to OCD's barriers.

The Importance of Goal-Setting in OCD Rehabilitation

1. Direction and Purpose:Goals characteristic as a compass, providing guidance and which means in the route of the way of restoration. They provide human beings a concrete aim to paintings for via the usage of outlining the moves they want to do to improve.

2. Autonomy and Empowerment: Establishing goals allows people to participate actively and independently of their non-public restoration. It moves the emphasis from the problems because of OCD to proactive measures imagined to sell non-public improvement and get beyond certain roadblocks.

three. Measurable Progress:Specific goals may be measured. Monitoring one's development gives people a tangible manner of spotting their accomplishments, so as to boom motivation and feelings of fulfillment.

four. Put Your Attention on Positivity:A brilliant outlook is aided via the use of goals. They inspire optimism and resiliency within the face of OCD-related problems with the useful resource of framing the restoration method in phrases of accomplishments and benchmarks.

5. Customization to Individual Needs:Creating desires permits a tailor-made technique for rehabilitation. Since absolutely all and sundry's experience with OCD is incredible,

defining desires primarily based on precise necessities and conditions makes the recovery plan more applicable and a hit.

Guidelines for Efficient Goal-Setting in OCD Rehabilitation:

1. Specific and Realistic: – Objectives should be every particular and all the way down to earth in truth. They want to explicitly find out capability measures that contribute to usual recuperation, in region of just summary objectives. For instance, figuring out to make a positive obsessive hobby a good buy much less commonplace.

2. Gradual Progression:This is an vital step. When greater bold goals are divided into more conceivable, smaller ones, humans can also furthermore growth continuously without feeling overburdened. Momentum is bolstered with the useful resource of little successes.

3. Prioritization:Set desires in order of significance and effect. Determining the most

vital components of recuperation ensures that belongings are allotted to regions an incredible manner to offer the maximum blessings.

4. Measurable Outcomes:To reveal development, set quantifiable dreams. Measurable effects offer readability, whether or not or not or not they may be used to expose the decrease in obsessive thoughts, the time elapsed among compulsive sports, or upgrades in famous nicely being.

5. Adaptability and Flexibility:Objectives want to be adaptive and bendy. Understand that recovery is a dynamic method, and that modifications can be required in response to shifting situations or growing awareness of 1's private requirements.

6. Add Behavioral techniques:Include behavioral strategies on your goals. Incorporate exposure and response prevention (ERP) strategies as unique sports activities within the goal-setting framework,

for instance, if the reason is to limit checking behavior.

7. Celebrate Success:Honor all your accomplishments, no matter how little. Acknowledging and applauding accomplishments encourage accurate behavior and increase force to pursue goals similarly.

The Transformational Effect of Well-Defined Objectives:

1. Enhanced Motivation:Motivation is increased with the useful resource of really stated dreams. The objectives' precision and clarity offer a avenue map that conjures up human beings to take an lively function of their rehabilitation, specially whilst subjects are difficult.

2. Decreased Anxiety:Setting dreams facilitates one sense in control and lessens anxiety associated with OCD's unpredictable nature. Reaching goals produces a nice

remarks loop that complements self guarantee and decreases fear.

three. Improved interest:By focusing interest on positive desires, purpose-placing complements cognizance. By that specialize in sensible solutions as opposed to the overpowering scope of OCD, this centered technique assists humans in navigating the contamination's intricacies.

4. Increased Resilience:Resilience is elevated through purpose-placing and accomplishment. Overcoming barriers, screw ups, or relapses is a critical a part of the journey that builds resilience and the functionality to keep moving into tough times.

five. Increased Coping Strategies:Setting and undertaking dreams gives an possibility to workout and decorate coping abilities. Behavioral methods, mindfulness, or exposure techniques—all of these provide opportunities for the ordinary use of beneficial coping mechanisms.

6. Change in Self-mind-set:Reaching desires encourages a top notch exchange in one's mind-set of oneself. People start to see themselves not as passive beneficiaries of remedy but as energetic people in their non-public healing, which enhances their feeling of self-efficacy.

7. Long-Term Perspective:Establishing dreams promotes a long-term outlook for rehabilitation. While short-term dreams help preserve attention, in addition they resource inside the formation of a extra entire information of lengthy-time period nicely-being and a life unencumbered through way of OCD.

Realistic Illustrations of OCD Rehab Objectives:

1. Minimizing Obsessive Distinctions:

Objective: Using publicity and response prevention techniques, little by little lower the frequency of a sure obsessive hobby (like handwashing) thru 20% over the route of the subsequent month.

2. Mindfulness Integration:Objective: Ten mins a day of mindfulness meditation to beautify reputation and cultivate a nonjudgmental mind-set inside the direction of compulsive thoughts.

3. Incremental Exposure Goals:Objective: Expose oneself to conditions that reason obsessive thoughts little by little, beginning with an entire lot less horrifying ones and going for walks one's way as much as greater hard ones.

four. Improving Daily Functioning:Objective: Improve every day functioning via assigning splendid duties or sports activities to do every day and then regularly broadening the scope as competence and self assurance growth.

5. Social Engagement Goals:Objective: Lessen social avoidance inclinations connected to OCD by using using growing social

engagement via taking element in a social hobby or occasion at least once every week.

Setting dreams is a dynamic and powerful method for OCD rehabilitation. Along with presenting a course forward, it moreover helps resilience, superior motivation, and a terrific outlook. Well-described goals with a basis in particular and capability outcomes might also additionally basically alter the path of remedy, guiding patients towards a lifestyles of harmony, because of this, and independence from the policies imposed via obsessive-compulsive sickness.

Chapter 17: Tracking Development And Modifying Approaches

A dynamic and successful method for treating obsessive-compulsive ailment (OCD) ought to embody tracking improvement and making crucial approach modifications. Effectively treating OCD signs and promoting lengthy-time period well-being calls for the capability to continuously evaluate development, modify techniques, and improve treatment plans. This research explores the significance of monitoring development and improving techniques within the context of OCD recuperation, highlighting the advantages of these techniques and giving guidelines on how people may additionally additionally control the continuous approach of enhancing their strategy.

Importance of Progress Monitoring:

1.   Objective   Assessment:Tracking improvement offers a methodical manner to assess the efficacy of selected treatments. It gives people the capability to evaluate if their

efforts are paying off and gives them a basis for clever selection-making.

2. Identifying Patterns:Consistent tracking allows the identity of patterns within the actions and symptoms of OCD. A greater entire knowledge of the contamination is feasible at the same time as precise triggers, variances in symptom severity, and variables affecting the frequency of compulsions are diagnosed.

3. Celebrating Achievements:Tracking enhancements offers a danger to renowned accomplishments. No rely how little, spotting and celebrating milestones encourages top conduct and boosts motivation and a feel of success.

four. Adaptability to Changing necessities:Over time, OCD signs and symptoms and personal requirements may additionally additionally alternate. By maintaining music of improvement, humans can also modify their plans in reaction to evolving conditions, preserving interventions present day and useful.

5. Motivation Feedback Loop:Developing a motivation remarks loop improves motivation. Seeing upgrades, tracking enhancements, and getting credit for work all feed proper right into a in no manner-finishing loop of belief that maintains humans pushing in advance with their healing.

Methods for Tracking Development:

1. Journaling:Keep a diary to document regular activities, triggers, and symptoms of OCD. Frequent postings assist end up privy to styles and tendencies during time through retaining song of accomplishments, screw ups, and insights.

2. Introspection:Practice introspection on a everyday foundation. Give careful attention to adjustments in cognitive patterns, emotional fitness, and the results of extremely good restoration strategies. A greater profound comprehension of 1's

studies is fostered thru sincere self-pondered picture.

3. Use of Rating Scales:To degree symptom depth and display screen modifications, use rating scales or questionnaires. This methodical technique offers a quantifiable manner of evaluating development and facilitating green communique with highbrow fitness experts.

4. Therapist Feedback:Consult therapists or one of a kind intellectual health professionals for their critiques. Frequent test-ins with the scientific frame of personnel taking detail within the treatment approach offer an unbiased viewpoint and insightful records on the patient's improvement.

five. Collaborative Conversations:Hold cooperative conversations with networks of help. A extra thorough assessment of development can be carried out with the aid of the usage of incorporating the insightful observations and grievance furnished with the useful aid of pals, own family, and assist business enterprise members.

Advantages of Modifying Techniques:

1. Tailored Interventions:Modifying processes allows interventions to be custom designed to fulfill the necessities of anybody. Individuals may moreover beautify their method and make remedies extra effective and individualized as they studies what works excellent for them.

2. Increased Effectiveness:By enhancing techniques in response to monitoring effects, the rehabilitation plan's common efficacy is raised. It ensures that interventions stay everyday with the needs of the prevailing and address converting troubles.

3. Prevention of Plateau:Consistent modifications protect in opposition to advancement plateauing. Due to the dynamic nature of OCD recuperation, it is important to frequently fight and conquer new elements of

the scenario with the intention to save you stagnation.

four.   Enhanced   Coping Mechanisms:Modifications useful resource the continuous increase of coping techniques. Through the technique of honing coping mechanisms, people turn out to be greater equipped to manage specific triggers, compulsive behaviors, and obsessive mind, which in turn builds resilience.

5.   Enhanced   Adherence   to treatment:Modifying strategies improves adherence to therapy. People are more likely to live with the method if they actively contribute to growing their recovery plan primarily based completely mostly on non-stop remarks.

Methods for Modifying Strategies:

1. Regular Review with Therapist:Make an appointment with a therapist to behavior regular critiques. Work collectively with the therapist to evaluate the affected individual's

development, talk via issues, and regulate the remedy plan as needed.

2. Incorporate New Techniques:Research and use sparkling techniques to remedy. Keep yourself updated on new findings and strategies, and be inclined to consist of different methods that during shape your tastes and necessities.

three. Input from Support Network:Consult the help community for enter. Friends, spouse and kids, or people of a aid agency could probable offer insightful comments on behavioral, emotional, and extremely-contemporary well-being adjustments.

four. Gradual Exposure Progression:Modify the publicity sporting events' development. To promote sustained improvement and model, recollect progressively elevating trouble if positive exposures begin to become a superb deal an awful lot less hard.

5.   Discover   Complementary
Methods:Examine   complementary

techniques. Incorporating supplementary methods like as mindfulness, rest techniques, or physical interest might also moreover decorate desired nicely-being and useful resource in OCD healing.

Handling Difficulties When Changing Techniques:

1. Patience and Flexibility:Exercise every of those virtues. Changing methods wishes being open to attempting new matters, paying attention to outcomes, and being adaptable to every achievements and failures.

2. Interaction with Experts:Continue to have candid discussions with intellectual health professionals. Talk about barriers, troubles, and any opposition to nice interventions so that you may additionally collectively investigate adjustments that in shape every person's requirements.

three. Self-Compassion:Develop compassion for yourself. Acknowledge that converting methods is an average factor of the recovery manner. When matters are changing, undergo in mind to cope with your self with kindness and see them as possibilities to beautify.

four. Appreciate Adaptability:Honor flexibility. Accept being capable of exchange tactics as a energy in place of a weak spot. A high great mentality is reinforced whilst modifications are visible as proactive movements within the route of advanced consequences.

As the approach of thrashing obsessive-compulsive illness maintains, monitoring development and enhancing strategies are critical and effective actions. These techniques enhance self-attention, guarantee the efficacy of remedy options, and help the improvement of a custom designed and robust strategy for OCD recuperation. People who be given that development is iterative manipulate the intricacies of the contamination with flexibility, tenacity, and a strength of will to prolonged-time period nicely-being.

Chapter 18: Handling Obstacles

A crucial element of the hard but lifestyles-converting technique of conquering obsessive-compulsive illness (OCD) is learning to address setbacks. In the restoration way, setbacks are inevitable, and overcoming them requires perseverance, self-compassion, and a calculated approach. This research explores how important it's far to control setbacks in the context of OCD recuperation, collectively with expertise of the individual of setbacks, coping mechanisms, and cultivating a mentality that encourages non-stop improvement.

Acknowledging Obstacles in OCD Rehabilitation:

1. OCD's Inherent Nature:OCD is inherently characterized through setbacks. Recurrent intrusive mind and compulsive actions are the sickness's hallmarks, and overcoming durations of prolonged anxiety, setbacks, and sporadic relapses is a part of the remedy manner.

2. Recovery Complexity:The system of having better from OCD is dynamic and complicated. People may additionally have troubles and disasters as they cope with unique triggers, entire exposure sports activities sports, and adapt to moving situations.

3. Learning Opportunities:Opportunities for reading rise up from setbacks. Examining setbacks may additionally display hidden reasons, untreated signs and symptoms and symptoms, or locations in which coping mechanisms need to be reinforced. Being proactive includes seeing boundaries as opportunities for development.

Techniques for Overcoming Setbacks:

1. Practice Self-Compassion:Develop self-compassion within the face of failures. Recognize that barriers are a vital a part of the restoration manner and workout self-compassion as opposed to self-criticism. Recognize the art work and enhancements performed, records that disasters do now not negate the improvement carried out.

2. Reevaluate and Adjust objectives:In the occasion of a setback, evaluation and adjust your targets as desired. Consider whether or now not or not the triumphing goals are affordable, available, and appropriate for anybody. Changes may additionally embody adjusting the price of development or going over positive strategies once more.

3. Seek Professional Guidance:Consult with intellectual fitness specialists. OCD-expert therapists can also provide insightful recommendation, a reevaluation of treatment strategies, and further coping mechanisms to help human beings deal with setbacks.

4. Involve Support Networks:Rely on networks of allies. Talk about failures with cherished ones, pals, or people in a guide organization. Since open conversation promotes empathy and statistics, it enables to create a supportive surroundings even inside the maximum attempting times.

five. Mindful Reflection:Take problem in reflective sports sports. Examine the motives of setbacks, along side stresses, triggers, or agenda modifications. By reflecting mindfully, one also can see trends and create plans to reduce the outcomes of incredible problems.

6. Incremental Progress:Pay hobby to little steps in advance. Divide the recovery method into smaller, greater feasible levels. Celebrate the perseverance proven within the face of problems and widely diagnosed the progress completed, mainly in the face of setbacks.

7. Practice Coping Strategies:Use coping techniques whilst faced with limitations. A toolbox of coping mechanisms, together with mindfulness, deep respiration physical sports activities, or grounding techniques, offers an prepared method of handling elevated tension and intrusive mind.